Oroonoko

"Imoinda" - Constructed character

Other playtexts recently published by Amber Lane Press include

SAMUEL ADAMSON
Clocks and Whistles
Grace Note

CARLO ARDITO
Brief Candle and Other Plays

'BIYI BANDELE
Death Catches the Hunter
Marching for Fausa
Resurrections
Two Horsemen

JULIAN MITCHELL
August
Falling Over England

ALAN PLATER
I Thought I Heard a Rustling

MARTIN SHERMAN
A Madhouse in Goa
Some Sunny Day

KUNIO SHIMIZU
Tango at the End of Winter

AUGUST STRINDBERG
The Father; Lady Julie; Playing with Fire
Motherly Love; Pariah; The First Warning

HUGH WHITEMORE
A Letter of Resignation
It's Ralph

For a free copy of our complete list of plays and theatre books write to:
Amber Lane Press, Church Street, Charlbury, Oxon OX7 3PR
Telephone and fax: 01608 810024

Aphra Behn's

Oroonoko

in a new adaptation by
'Biyi Bandele

AMBER LANE PRESS

All rights whatsoever in this play are strictly reserved
and application for professional or amateur performance
should be made before rehearsals begin to:
The Agency (London) Ltd
24 Pottery Lane
Holland Park
London W11 4LZ
No performance may be given unless a licence has been
obtained.

First published in 1999 by
Amber Lane Press Ltd.
Church Street
Charlbury
Oxford OX7 3PR
Telephone: 01608 810024

Printed and bound by
The Guernsey Press Co. Ltd., Guernsey, C.I.

ISBN: 1 872868 25 8

Foreword

It is said of Eshu, the Yoruba trickster-God, who is the ubiquitous reverse hero of *Oroonoko*, that 'he threw a rock today, and killed a bird yesterday.' In other words, what is to happen in the future is the cause of what is happening now. The present, says this paradox, is defined by the future. Eshu, and his metaphor of transcendence has inspired this feast-of-a-war – which is to say jam session – between a myth and two mythmakers situated three hundred years apart. Together they contemplate a past that resonates in its future. A past that is forever echoed, distorted, amplified, invoked and interrogated by the present.

The African kingdom known to Europeans as Coramantien existed in what is known today as Ghana. But Aphra Behn's Coramantien is a notional one. I have situated the first part of my re-imagined *Oroonoko* in a Yoruba – which is to say Nigerian – setting chiefly beause the characters in Behn's novel bear names that are recognisably Yoruba. Ultimately, though, Coramantien, our fabled kingdom, is born of a distilled evocation of a metaphorical megalopolis of intersecting universal dreams.

'Biyi Bandele
London, 1999

Preface

oxymoron

In 1688 the British writer and playwright Aphra Behn published her 'true history' called *Oroonoko: or The Royal Slave.* It tells the story of an African prince, tricked into slavery and separated from his love, Princess Imoinda. Oroonoko ends up in the British colony of Surinam on the northeast coast of South America, where he is persuaded to lead a slave revolt. The uprising fails and he is executed.

Aphra Behn claims to have known Oroonoko, and to have been an eye-witness to many of the events in her narrative. She certainly appears to have spent some of her young life in Surinam, although this, like many of the details of her life, is difficult to verify. In *Oroonoko* she states:

> I do not pretend, in giving you the History of this Royal Slave, to entertain my reader with the Adventures of a feign'd Hero, whose Life and Fortunes Fancy may manage at the Poet's Pleasure; nor in relating the Truth, design to adorn it with any Accidents, but such as arriv'd in earnest to him: And it shall come simply in the World, recommended by its own proper Merits, and natural Intrigues; there being enough of Reality to support it, and to render it diverting, without the Addition of Invention.

Her purpose in writing down her account of the African prince was, she said, 'to make his Glorious Name survive all Ages.'

Behn died in 1689, the year after the publication of *Oroonoko*. She never adapted it for the stage herself. The playwright Thomas Southerne wondered why.

> Mrs Behn had a great command of the stage; and I have often wonder'd that she would bury her Favourite Hero in a *Novel*, when she might have reviv'd him in the *Scene*. She thought either that no Actor could represent him; or she could not bear him represented. And I believe the last,

7

when I remember what I have heard from a Friend of hers, That she always told his Story more feelingly than she writ it.

In 1695 Southerne's own adaptation received its first performance. It continued to hold the stage throughout the eighteenth century.

The young David Garrick appeared in *Oroonoko* as Aboan, in a touring production in Ipswich in 1741, and later revised the play, cutting out the silly subplot and heightening the tragedy. In the Prologue to his own version he wrote:

This Night your Tributary Tears we claim,
For Scenes that Southerne drew; a fav'rite name!
He touch'd your Father's Hearts with gen'rous Woe
And taught your Mother's youthful Eyes to flow . . .
Yet, Slave to Custom in a laughing Age,
With ribald Mirth he stain'd the sacred Page.

In February 1749 two African princes, guests of the Earl of Halifax, visited Covent Garden to see the play, and the occasion was reported in the *Gentleman's Magazine*:

They were received with a loud clap of applause, which they acknowledged with a very genteel bow, and took their seats in a box. Then seeing persons of their own colour on the stage, apparently in the same distress from which they had been so lately delivered, the tender interview between Imoinda and Oroonoko, his account of his sufferings, and the repeated abuse of his placability and confidence, strongly affected them with that generous grief which pure native always feels, and which art had not yet taught them to suppress; the young prince was so far overcome, that he was obliged to retire at the end of the fourth act. His companion remained but wept the whole time, a circumstance which affected the audience yet more than the play.

From the late 1750s Garrick's version, and others, showed a more pronounced anti-slavery feeling, and the play became increasingly popular with the abolitionist movement.

8

Until now, stage adaptations of Aphra Behn's novella have concentrated on the story of Oroonoko's arrival in Surinam, his interaction with the British colonists and slave traders, and his part in the mutiny which brought about his death.

In this version for the RSC, 'Biyi Bandele brings both halves of his hero's story together, from warrior and prince in the West African Kingdom of Coramantien to slave in Surinam. This is the first time, therefore, that Oroonoko's entire story has been presented on the stage.

Gregory Doran
Stratford-upon-Avon, 1999

Oroonoko was first performed by the Royal Shakespeare Company at The Other Place, Stratford-upon-Avon, on 7 April 1999.

The cast was as follows:

Israel Aduramo ... LAYE
Rod Arthur ... CAPTAIN STANMORE
Kemi Baruwa ... BOLA
David Collings ... BYAM
Ewen Cummins ... OTMAN
Michael Fenner ... TREFRY
Geff Francis ... OROMBO
Nadine Marshall ... IMOINDA
Jo Martin ... LADY ONOLA
Nicholas Monu ... OROONOKO
David Oyelowo ... ABOAN
Farimang Singhateh ... ROYAL DRUMMER
Ewart James Walters ... AKOGUN/KABIYESI

Nicky Reid ... Percussion

Other parts played by members of the company

Directed by Gregory Doran
Designed by Niki Turner
Lighting designed by Tim Mitchell
Music by Juwon Ogungbe
Movement by Alex Oma-Pius
Fights by Terry King
Sound by Martin Slavin
Company voice work by Andrew Wade and Cicely Berry
Production Manager Mark Graham
Costume Supervisor Jenny Alden

Stage Manager Diana Stalker
Deputy Stage Manager Pip Horobin
Assistant Stage Manager Joanna Stone

Dramatis Personae *in a Novella*

Part One: Coramantien

Oroonoko, the Prince
Aboan, his friend
Laye, his friend
Imoinda, the Princess
Lady Onola, her adoptive mother
Akogun, a General
Kabiyesi, the King of Coramantien
Chief Orombo, the King's chief adviser
Bola, Orombo's daughter
Ibn Saeed, an emissary of war
Ibn Sule, an emissary of war
Captain Green, an English sailor
Captain Stanmore, an English sailor

Various warriors, musicians, servants, crews, & other persons

Part Two: Surinam

Oroonoko
Aboan
Imoinda
Mr Trefry
Mr Byam, Deputy Governor of Surinam
Captain Stanmore
Otman, a slave

Various slaves, planters, Indians & other persons

11

PART ONE

CORAMANTIEN

Act One

Scene 1

The main court of the palace of the KABIYESI, *King of Coramantien. Although we do not see the King we are immediately made aware of his presence through the gathering of* MINISTERS, GUARDS *and* COURTIERS, *whose gaze, to a man, is focused in one direction: towards the King's antechamber, which is concealed behind an elaborately draped door at one end of the richly embroidered mat stretching across the court.*

OROONOKO, *a powerfully built young man in his late teens, is standing immediately behind the* AKOGUN, *the Generalissimo, head of the kingdom's armed forces, whose face, inscrutable, is focused on two visitors standing in the centre of the court.*

Although the visitors, IBN SAEED *and* IBN SULE, *are, like their hosts, Africans, they are dressed in turbans and other such accoutrements of the desert-farer: clothing that immediately marks them apart from the people of Coramantien, who are dressed in the coastal Yoruba style of 'agbada' and 'dashiki'.*

IBN SAEED *is reading out loud a letter written, in Arabic script, on a scroll of parchment.*

IBN SAEED   To sum up: if you respond to the oath
Of allegiance and to its conditions –
Namely, that you expel into the wild all
Those of our enemies who come to your
Land, and that you allow free passage
To all the people of the kingdoms which
Lie beyond you who have come to enter
Into obedience to us – which is an obligatory
Duty for both them and you, then you
And your subjects and your lands are safe
And secure, protected by our mercy which
Shall guard you from all sides so that you
Shall not experience from our Exalted Abode

15

Anything which shall harm you or alarm
You to the end of time, if it be the will of God;
You shall be safe and secure, and you shall
Have support from our divinely
Victorious armies over your enemies.

But if you refuse to respond
And your bad judgement causes you
To deviate from the path of success,
Then receive the glad tidings of our
Conquering armies aided by God and
Our extensive military forces made
Victorious by God, which shall pour over
Your land from Kebbi – if God wills,
Like torrential floodwater or the raging sea.
You will think it a downpour flowing with
Ignominy and destruction, until
By God's might, they shall reduce your
Land to a barren wilderness and bring
You to the same plight as the erstwhile
Monarch of your neighbours, the Kitipa,
Whom they made to taste death and whom
Together with his kingdom they swallowed up,
Since he had disobeyed our Exalted Command.
We have given you fair warning and notice.
So choose yourself and pursue the path
Which your better judgement commends.
Peace.

> [*A charged silence ensues as* IBN SAEED *carefully and
> fastidiously folds the scroll, betraying, for the first
> time, his tension by tugging absentmindedly at his
> sword and looking to* IBN SULE *for guidance.* IBN SULE
> *directs a bow at the draped door of the antechamber.*]

IBN SULE   Your Highness, that is the message to you
            From our Lord and Master,
            His Exalted Eminence the King of Kebbi,
            El Hadj Sani Farouk,

Messenger of the Prophet,
Defender of the Faithful,
Teacher of Teachers,
Conquering Sovereign of the Desert Country,
Of whom it is said, 'The sandstorm is the answer
To the man wearing a rain-coat,' because
He descends upon his enemies with
The blinding ferocity of a desert storm.
He requires an immediate response.
He sends felicitations.

> [*The* AKOGUN, *who is positioned nearest to the ante-chamber, leans forward and listens to instructions from the* KABIYESI. *The instructions are short. The* AKOGUN *bows and nods, then turns to the visitors with great formality.*]

AKOGUN His Royal Highness, the Kabiyesi –
Long may he reign –
IBN SULE Long indeed may he reign.
AKOGUN – Wishes to confer in private
With you, Ibn Sule.
IBN SULE Very well, General.

> [IBN SULE *walks towards the door, which the* AKOGUN *is now holding ajar.*]

AKOGUN Oroonoko.
OROONOKO Yes, my Lord.
AKOGUN Follow me.
OROONOKO Yes, my Lord.

> [*Exit* IBN SULE, OROONOKO *and the veteran* AKOGUN.]

> [*There is a long silence during which* IBN SAEED *tries not to fidget. Then – offstage – a sharp, abbreviated scream lasting no longer than a second.* IBN SAEED *starts. His body sags. He goes completely ashen.*]

> [*Enter the* AKOGUN, *followed by* OROONOKO.]

> [*The drumming stops as abruptly as it began.*]

[*The* AKOGUN *approaches* IBN SAEED.]

AKOGUN   His Highness had a most lively
Palaver with Ibn Sule. They talked
About many things: the fluctuating price
Of salt, the constellations, the trade in slaves.
Ibn Sule even entertained His Highness
With a joke whose punch-line escapes
Me now. Something about a Portuguese
Tailor. Or perhaps he said sailor.
Let me assure you, though:
His Highness did not forget to laugh.

IBN SAEED   [*fidgets*] Where is Ibn Sule?

AKOGUN   Your brother-messenger desired a shave –

IBN SAEED   [*his heart skipping a beat*] A sh–shave?

AKOGUN   Yes, a shave. Luckily for him
The Royal Barber was at hand.

[*He snaps his fingers.* OROONOKO *reveals the content of the sack. It is* IBN SULE's *head.*]

AKOGUN   As you can see the beard
Is unlikely to grow back.

[IBN SAEED *stares in stunned silence at his beheaded colleague.*]

AKOGUN   Your master required an immediate
Response to his petition. His Highness,
The Kabiyesi –

OROONOKO   – Long may he reign –

AKOGUN   – Long may he reign – is a
Courteous man, he loathes to keep people
Waiting. He wants you to take this head
Back to your master without delay.
He begs you to pass on the following message:
We know that the gods, in their great wisdom
Or for amusement, sometimes give nuts
To those that have no teeth. But a joke is a
Joke. Should ever your master take leave of his senses

Again, should he ever slur our land with
Such discourtesy again, we shall walk
All the way to his palace, drag him out on to the
Pestilential wilderness of his sand-strewn
Kingdom, and shave his beard for him.
Ibn Sule's clean-shaven chin
Will testify to the sureness of our touch.
That is my King's message to your master,
Ibn Saeed. Go, Ibn Saeed,
And as you go, dwell on this truth
Which it has pleased His Highness to share
With you: this earth is great, and so is our kingdom.

Scene 2

A military camp on the outskirts of Coramantien.

OROONOKO *is busy re-stringing his bow.*

Enter ABOAN, LAYE, *and several other* CONSCRIPTS *carrying drums. They run to* OROONOKO *and drag him up.*

OROONOKO	Oh no.
LAYE	Oh yes, Oroonoko. You're
	Playing the Old Sage.
OROONOKO	No, I'm not.
LAYE	Yes, you are.
OROONOKO	Leave me alone, Laye.
LAYE	Come on, Oroonoko.
	Don't be an elephant's fart.
OROONOKO	If the General catches us.
LAYE	The General won't catch us.
	The General is at the palace
	Attending a meeting of the War Council.
OROONOKO	Precisely what I'm saying.
	We are on the brink of war.
	This is no time for games.
LAYE	And what happens when
	There's war?

OROONOKO	Your gallant father's long-lost Backache suddenly reappears. What Do you think happens when There's war?
LAYE	People die.
OROONOKO	Deep thinking.
ABOAN	That's not thinking. That's what Thinking *becomes*.
OROONOKO	I was being sarcastic, Aboan.
ABOAN	So was I, Oroonoko.

[OROONOKO *drops his bow*.]

OROONOKO	Alright, alright. But I do This under duress.

[*He stands up, and as he does so, he contorts his body into the shape of an infirm, but 'very wise' old man leaning on a walking stick.* LAYE, ABOAN *and the others gather around him and hold their drums at the ready.*]

ALL	You danced, Old Sage, You definitely danced!
OROONOKO	[*as the Old Sage*] I didn't, I didn't!
ALL	Oh yes, you danced! You danced, you danced!
OROONOKO	I didn't, I didn't!
ALL	Go home and tell them The Old Sage danced!
OROONOKO	I didn't, I didn't!
ALL	You danced, Old Sage, You definitely danced!
OROONOKO	Look at my beard: It's grey and thinning!
ALL	You danced, Old Sage, You definitely danced!
OROONOKO	Look at my eyes: All rheumy and sightless!

ALL	You danced, you danced!
	You definitely danced!
OROONOKO	Look at my arms, trembling,
	Just trembling!
ALL	You danced, Old Sage,
	You definitely danced!
OROONOKO	Look at my feet,
	I can hardly walk!
ALL	You danced, you danced!
	You definitely danced!
OROONOKO	Alright then, I'll have a go!

[*The drumming, mock sensual, commences and the 'Old Sage' starts dancing, slowly and clumsily at first, then as the drumming gathers pace, energetically and with great skill. Soon, OROONOKO is so absorbed in the role, not just his ears but his eyes as well are closed to all else.*]

[*The other youths, ever vigilant, spot the AKOGUN from afar.*]

[*Enter the AKOGUN.*]

[*Exit LAYE and ABOAN and the other CONSCRIPTS.*]

[*OROONOKO continues dancing even after the drumming has ceased.*]

[*The AKOGUN watches him with bemused interest.*]

AKOGUN	[*barks*] Oroonoko!

[*OROONOKO practically jumps out of his skin.*]

OROONOKO	My Lord!
AKOGUN	What exactly do you
	Think you're doing,
	Oroonoko?
OROONOKO	I . . . we were playing
	'Old Sage You Danced.'
AKOGUN	Old-who-you-what?

OROONOKO   'Old Sage You Danced.'

                 [*The* AKOGUN *picks up* OROONOKO's *broken bow.*]

AKOGUN   I see. Remind me, Oroonoko,
            What were you meant to be doing
            Out here in the Forest of Demons?

OROONOKO   [*gruff with embarrassment*] Training, sir . . . my Lord.

AKOGUN   Training to be what?

OROONOKO   Warriors, my Lord.

AKOGUN   Training to be a warrior.
            That's right. This is a military
            Training ground, not a playground
            For court jesters, Oroonoko.

OROONOKO   Yes, my Lord.
            They forced me, my Lord.
            I didn't want to join in, my Lord.

AKOGUN   It wasn't your idea. 'They'
            Forced you. You disappoint me,
            Oroonoko. Let me remind you of
            The story of the five fingers –

OROONOKO   The five fingers, my Lord?

AKOGUN   The first finger said: I'm hungry.
            The second finger said: I'm broke.
            The third finger said: Let's steal some mangoes.
            The fourth finger said: And if the farmer catches us?
            The fifth finger said: Go and steal; I'll stand apart.
            That is the story of the five fingers, Oroonoko.

OROONOKO   I'm sure, my Lord.

AKOGUN   Each finger had a choice.
            Each finger made a choice.

OROONOKO   Yes, my Lord.

AKOGUN   Nobody forces you to do a thing,
            Oroonoko. Let me attempt to tell
            You why: His Highness, the King –

OROONOKO   – Long may he reign –

AKOGUN   – Long may he reign – the King
            Is now getting on in years. In his younger
            Days, he had many sons, thirteen in all.

Now he has none: they all died in battle,
Conquering when they fell.
I fought alongside those gallant heroes.
I cherish the memory of their bravery.
Now, the King has left for him for his
Successor, one grandchild, son to one
Of these dead victors. This grandchild,
As soon as he could walk, was sent into the
Field to be trained by one of the King's most
Experienced Generals. And from his natural
Inclination to arms, and the occasions of war
Given him, and – we believe, with the good
Conduct of the old General, the boy became,
At the age of seventeen, one of the kingdom's
Most expert captains. Am I getting through
To you, Oroonoko?

OROONOKO   Yes, my Lord.

AKOGUN   You are a prince, Oroonoko.
The heir apparent to the throne
Of our land, a king-in-waiting.
You have already proved your
Bravery in war. I was there when
You claimed your first scalp, just
As I was when your father,
Abiodun – may he guide you from
The land of the ancestors –
Slew his first man. He was born
A leader, your father, a prince
Among men. And so are you,
Oroonoko. But to be a leader,
It is not enough to excel as a
Warrior. That, and more is required:
To be a leader, you have to lead,
And leadership me⬤ taking responsibility.
It was bad enough that you
Took part in that childish game.
That was the least of it. But to try
And evade responsibility. . .

OROONOKO   Forgive me, my Lord.
AKOGUN   There's nothing to forgive.
           But do remember this,
           My king-in-the-making:
           'I entered but took nothing,'
           Will not save the thief.

> [*He hands the broken bow back to* OROONOKO.]

AKOGUN   Hurry up with that bow, warrior.
OROONOKO   [*expectantly*] My Lord?
AKOGUN   The War Council has decided.
           We are going to war.

> [*Exit the* AKOGUN.]

Scene 3

The military training ground.

Enter ABOAN, LAYE *and the other* TRAINEES.

LAYE   [*in exasperation.*] War? I thought we had a
           Peace treaty with those animals.
           I thought it said, 'no more war.'
ABOAN   It does say no more war.
           That's why it's called a peace treaty.
OROONOKO   But now they are violating
           The rules of engagement.
LAYE   Rules? What rules?
           I thought it simply says:
           'No more war!'
ABOAN   Not that simply, it doesn't.
LAYE   I've had enough of your
           Lip for one day, Aboan.
           War! I hate it.
OROONOKO   Why?
LAYE   It interferes with my social calendar.
ABOAN   What social calendar?

LAYE   The one that mentions
         Your mother and me
         In bed together.
ABOAN   Come here. What's that
         In your eye?
LAYE   What?
ABOAN   My fist.

> [*He hits* LAYE. LAYE *flings himself at* ABOAN. *They wrestle.*]

Scene 4

The battlefield.

Enter the WARRIORS *of Coramantien and their* ENEMIES.

A fierce hand-to-hand battle rages. Bodies fall to the ground like so many leaves. OROONOKO *excels, cutting through the enemy with ease, and slaying them as they accost him.*

Exit ABOAN *pursued by an enemy.*

Exit LAYE *pursuing the enemy.*

Exit an enemy pursuing LAYE.

OROONOKO *sees that the* AKOGUN *is outnumbered. He rushes to his aid. Together, they see off the attackers, but the* AKOGUN *is fatally wounded.* OROONOKO *holds him in his arms, as he lies dying.*

The battle rages on all around them.

OROONOKO   Persevere, my General.
            This battle will soon be over.
            I beg of you, hang in there.
AKOGUN   It's no use, my king-in-waiting,
            That savage's arrow has sliced
            Through parts of my body I
            Didn't even know existed. I'm dying,
            My fellow warrior.
OROONOKO   [*emotionally*] You will not die, my General.
            You will see this through.

[*Enter* LAYE, *with a knife embedded in the back of his skull. He is leaning on to* ABOAN, *who is slightly wounded.*]

LAYE   [*ecstatic*] Tell him, Aboan. Tell Oroonoko
          How I nailed those bastards.

ABOAN   The savages had me cornered.
          Laye saved my life.

LAYE   [*swaggers*] I sent them screaming to the
          Dunghill of their ancestors.

OROONOKO [*disconsolate*] Laye, Laye.

LAYE   [*collapses.*] They've killed me, Oroonoko.
          Those bastards have killed me.

          [*He dies.*]

AKOGUN   Promise me, Oroonoko,
          That you'll look after my daughter Imoinda.
          She is a child that must
          Not be touched by dew. And since
          Her mother died so long ago, she
          Has been the light with which I've
          Found my way. Promise me, Oroonoko
          That you will look after her for me.

OROONOKO Upon this earth, my General,
          Upon this earth, I pledge you
          My word that as long as there's breath
          In me, Imoinda will want for nothing.

AKOGUN   You left the palace a lad, you go back
          A leader of men. Be careful when you go.
          The King is old, his grip on the
          Reins of power has grown shaky. But do not
          Be fooled, do not be in a hurry to succeed
          The throne. Help me up, Oroonoko,
          Prop me up on my feet. Let me walk
          Up to my ancestors.

          [*He dies.*]

Act Two

Scene 1

The King's palace in Coramantien.

Enter OROONOKO *and* ABOAN, *lately returned from the wars.*

OROONOKO *approaches* OROMBO, *chief adviser to the King.*

OROONOKO	Does His Highness know I'm here?
OROMBO	He knows.
OROONOKO	Will he be long in coming?
OROMBO	[*coolly*] His Highness will take as long as It takes for him to come.
OROONOKO	We could come back later. It's been a long trek And we haven't had a wash.
OROMBO	I share your interest in personal Hygiene. Have you tried soap? It's the new invention. My wives Swear by it.

[*Enter* LADY ONOLA, *a middle-aged courtesan.*]

OROMBO	Look, General, there's nothing I can do. His Highness is attending To eminently urgent affairs of the state.
ONOLA	Affairs of the state? Did you say Affairs of the state? [*to* OROONOKO] What Chief Orombo means is that His Highness our dear King is keeping His visitors waiting while he attempts To insert his Royal Privilege Into the comely virtues of a young maiden. Much ado – dare I say – over nothing. Were the King's penis a warrior – he Wishes it were – it would have been beheaded Long ago for persistent dereliction of duty.

OROMBO [*to* OROONOKO] Let me introduce you to Lady Onola.
        She is an abandoned mistress of
        His Highness.

ONOLA   It is well known in the seraglio
        That though the King never can
        Sleep, his penis is forever nodding off.

OROMBO [*indignantly*] Two of my own wives have had the rare
        Privilege of supping with the King. And
        Upon their word – they have no reason to lie –

ONOLA   – They do lie – with every boy-slave in the land.

OROMBO [*chokes*] – Upon their word, the Royal Manhood is as
        Long as the Royal Python.

ONOLA   Your wives may have slept with a snake,
        Chief Orombo, but not with the one
        Between the King's legs. It is a worm
        Bereft of limb, flattered into thinking
        Itself a reptile.

OROMBO How dare you, Lady Onola!
        How dare you!

ONOLA   I did tell your second wife, Kemi, when she said
        She was marrying you that you had not
        Done badly by her, for she is beautiful and
        So is her smile. You bedecked her with gold and bales
        Of cloth. But I could see, from looking at you,
        That you could not satisfy her in bed. What
        She needed in bed – I told her – was a man who once he
        Mounted her would not let off until the roof fell
        Through. Not a glorified pimp who farms out
        His wives and children to curry royal favour.

OROMBO [*stiffly*] It's called loyalty, Lady Onola, which
        Comes from Good Breeding. Have you
        Heard of Good Breeding? Ah, there I go again.
        Forgive me. Just like me to forget that you
        Were bred in a bordello.
        In any case I don't see how what I do or choose not to
        Do with my family is any of your business. And we are
        Talking not about me but about the Royal Manhood.
        Help me out, Praise-Singers!

1ST ROYAL DRUMMER   It is as your wives say, Chief Orombo,
                      The Royal *Thing* is long indeed.
2ND ROYAL DRUMMER   We haven't had a chance to size it up.
1ST ROYAL DRUMMER   But it's either very long –
2ND ROYAL DRUMMER   Or as long as it is!

        [OROMBO *glares stonily at them.*]

2ND ROYAL DRUMMER   His Highness – long may he reign –
                      Fathered a child in Liverpool
                      While emptying his testicles
                      In Coramantien!
    OROMBO [*to* ONOLA] You see? You see?
1ST ROYAL DRUMMER   That is not all. When once His Highness
                      Took the Royal Cock for a constitutional
                      In the marketplace –
2ND ROYAL DRUMMER   It sought the welcoming thighs of
                      A barren woman.
1ST ROYAL DRUMMER   The King entered deeply, deeply.
2ND ROYAL DRUMMER   He moved this way,
1ST ROYAL DRUMMER   And that way,
2ND ROYAL DRUMMER   And then straight on.
1ST ROYAL DRUMMER   Like an intrepid hunter running –
2ND ROYAL DRUMMER   – Then slowing down –
1ST ROYAL DRUMMER   – And then running again.
2ND ROYAL DRUMMER   He entered deeply, deeply.
                      He touched the base of his cock –
1ST ROYAL DRUMMER   –Was it asleep? Was it fatigued?
2ND ROYAL DRUMMER   He found that his cock, the fearless
                      Rogue, was not fatigued.
1ST ROYAL DRUMMER   It was thrusting, thrusting.
2ND ROYAL DRUMMER   Except for his testicles.
1ST ROYAL DRUMMER   Except for his testicles
                      Which were emptying.
    OROMBO [*to* ONOLA] You see? You see?
1ST ROYAL DRUMMER   His Highness shivered and screamed.
2ND ROYAL DRUMMER   The barren woman shivered and
                                        screamed.
1ST ROYAL DRUMMER   The King shivered and screamed.

2ND ROYAL DRUMMER   The woman shivered and screamed.
1ST ROYAL DRUMMER   She birthed twins nine months later.
    OROMBO [*delirious*] You see? You see?
2ND ROYAL DRUMMER   She had twins nine months later,
                     Yet the Royal Cock still hung rigid –
1ST ROYAL DRUMMER   Dripping thick, sticky tears –
2ND ROYAL DRUMMER   Was it from joy?
1ST ROYAL DRUMMER   Was it from pain?
2ND ROYAL DRUMMER   When we asked it why it was crying –
1ST ROYAL DRUMMER   The King's cock said,
2ND ROYAL DRUMMER   [as '*the King's cock*'] 'Crying? Crying?
                     Who said I was crying? This is how we
                     Grin, where I come from.'
    OROMBO You see? You see?
     ONOLA I did not come here to listen to the
            Idle prattle of jesters and eunuchs. As for
            The King – if you want my opinion –
            The problem with His Highness is that
            His brain is in his penis. More's
            The pity, since he has no penis.
    OROMBO I'm warning you, Lady Onola!
            I'm warning you!
     ONOLA Run along now. I did not come here to see you.
            I came here to see these strapping
            Warriors for myself. Word reached me
            They had come to pay homage to the
            Kabiyesi. Welcome home, young warriors,
            Your reputation precedes you like the crackling
            Roar of a bush-fire. And you, my Lord Oroonoko,
            You have a message from the Princess Imoinda, most
            Esteemed daughter of our late Generalissimo. She
            Heard that you were with her father when he breathed
            His last. If you would care to honour my compound this
            Evening with a visit, she will be there waiting to thank
            You in person.
            [*eyes* ABOAN]
            There's no reason of course why your gallant friend
            Shouldn't come along. The more the merrier.

[*Exit* LADY ONOLA.]

[*Enter* KABIYESI *the King. He is old and infirm, and practically carried to his throne by two* HELPERS. *He appears to be drunk, and is trying, rather ineffectually, to re-knot the belt-string of his trousers.*]

[OROONOKO *and* ABOAN *exchange looks. They prostrate themselves in greeting.* OROMBO *does likewise and more.*]

OROMBO   [*chants*] I salute you, my King:
You are, like a needle,
Sharp at both ends.

You pick your teeth with a sword.
Any mortal who scoffs at you
Will use his teeth in place of a knife
To peel cassava.

I am addressing you, my master:
You are the swift warrior moving
To battle in the enemy's bush path.

You are the waddling warrior
Cautiously advancing in enemy territory.

I pay you homage, my King.
You are a torrent of rainwater:
You go everywhere.

You are the forest fire that destroys the undergrowth
Together with the mass of leaves under it.

I salute you, my King.

[*The* KABIYESI *is still struggling with his trousers.*]

[*Enter a young woman,* BOLA, *from the King's chambers. She is distressed and weeping.*]

KABIYESI   Orombo!
OROMBO   Kabiyesi!

KABIYESI   Why do you insist on
            Bringing me these passionless hags?

            [OROMBO *eyes the distressed* BOLA.]

OROMBO   [*choosing his words carefully*]
            Kabiyesi, she's only. . .sixteen.
KABIYESI   *Only* sixteen – ?
OROMBO   Which, I admit, is getting on quite a bit.
KABIYESI   Only sixteen?
            Do you contradict me?
OROMBO   Oh no, Kabiyesi! I was merely trying
            To say . . . I know her age . . .
            She is my daughter.
KABIYESI   She may well be your daughter, Orombo,
            She behaves like your very own grandmother.
            I need young blood.
            Go and find me a winsome young virgin.
OROMBO   But, Kabiyesi –
KABIYESI   Go.
OROMBO   Yes, Kabiyesi.
            [*to* BOLA] You have disgraced us, Bola, you have ruined
            The good name of our family. We'll never
            Hear the end of it. Wait till your mother
            Hears about it. All you had to do was lie
            Back and think of our good name.

            [*Exit* OROMBO *with* BOLA.]

OROMBO   [*off*] Is that too much to ask of a daughter?
BOLA   [*off*] But father, I'm with child.
OROMBO   [*off*] With child?
            [*shouts*] With child?
BOLA   [*off*] Father –
OROMBO   [*off*] Take me to the wretch
            Who did this to you!
OROONOKO   Oroonoko, my King –
KABIYESI   Oroonoko! Come forward and embrace
            An old man. My gallant General,
            You have grown into a man.

[OROONOKO *embraces him.*]

KABIYESI I feel all alone, Oroonoko. I'm blind in one eye,
Deaf in one ear, and I'm losing my looks.
My ministers all are plotting against me.
And against one another. I am surrounded by
Spineless fools and sycophants. Do you think
I should secede?

OROONOKO A thousand needles do not make an axe, Kabiyesi.
A thousand wells do not make an ocean.
The earthworm cannot impersonate a snake –

[*The* KABIYESI *raises his eyebrows.* OROONOKO
quickly goes on:]

OROONOKO A man whose father is alive cannot be king.
Whether the moon shines or not, my father, my King –
You shine in the dark.

[*The* KABIYESI *laughs, flattered. His* COURTIERS *titter
nervously.*]

KABIYESI You are wise beyond your years, Oroonoko, you
May yet survive the intrigues of this place.

A rot-infected yam does not
Harm the knife used in cutting off the rot.
Go, Oroonoko, and weed out the rot in our kingdom.

Scene 2

A slave port.

A group of SLAVES, *all shackled together.*

Enter OROMBO *and* CAPTAIN GREEN, *an Englishman.*

GREEN *examines the slaves one by one. His method of examination involves
opening their mouths, checking their dentition and tongues, checking their
hair, their backs, and often their private parts.*

OROMBO Don't thank me until you've
Finished examining them.

GREEN Where do they come from?

OROMBO The King's own personal collection.
Where else do you imagine they come
From, my dear Captain Brown?

GREEN Green. The name is Green.

OROMBO Of course it is. Of course it is.
You very well know, my good friend, that
I deal only in the very best cargo.
No runny-nosed, sore-infested wretches from me.
No diseased items, no lazy, malnourished
Shipments. I bring you, my good friend,
Only the best. You see, I have done the King
Many a favour over the years.

OROMBO AND GREEN [*together*] I scratch your back –

OROMBO – You scratch mine.
I am that sort of man.
His Highness has rewarded
My enduring loyalty by granting me exclusive
Licence to administer the royal supply of slaves.
That means I sell them on his behalf:
I do all the work, he takes ninety
Percent of the proceeds –
And why shouldn't he? I am by
Definition his slave as well –
And everybody's happy. Except of course
For the slaves themselves.

This supply came in
Only this morning. The King's
Grandson, a brave man –
May the gods make a lesson of him,
Or surely I'm finished –
Commander-in-Chief of our brave warriors –
Took them captive from the theatre
Of war. They hail from a race of
Fierce warriors and hunters –
You
Can see that from their torsos

– From
The interior. They are hard workers
And in great demand. In normal
Times they would be kept in
The palace and trained to be attendants,
Guards – that sort of thing. But these are
Not normal times. Times are hard,
The King's coffers are not what they
Used to be, and – my dear Captain
Brown –

GREEN   Green.

OROMBO   – My good friend,
One is used to a certain standard
Of living.

Scene 3

LADY ONOLA*'s household.*

LADY ONOLA, PRINCESS IMOINDA *and several* SERVANTS *are there.*

Enter OROONOKO, *followed by* ABOAN.

ONOLA   Ladies. My friends and workers.
Sisters, let me present to you the
Mighty Oroonoko, in praise of
Whose patron God, Eshu, the God
Of fate, it has been said that:

When he stands up
Even a day-old suckling
Beggars him in height.
But when he lies down, the world
Clambers mountains to catch
Sight of his face.

Eshu slept in the house –
But the house was too
Small for him.

Eshu slept out in the open –
But the open was too
Small for him.

Eshu slept in a nut –
At last he could stretch himself!

Oroonoko, you're the jewel
Of your God's eye:
Did you not drive back
To their farthest borders
The galloping army of the Kebbi?

You worked havoc in the
Hinterland, stalking forth
Like a God aggrieved.

You did not spare the cities
Nor the rivers, nor farms
Nor the markets.

Your campaigns have
Been a matchless triumph
In the path of your God.

You are –
Our hero.
You are –
Oroonoko. We welcome you
And your brother-warriors.

OROONOKO   We thank you, our mother.
You are –
The thorn in the rhino's foot.
The pebble that breaks the leopard's tooth.
The rope that drags the elephant along.
The back that carries its brother.
The leaf that is bigger than a forest.

The hare that climbs a mountain running.
The sea that cannot be emptied.
The flood that struts through fire.
The silence that births a song.
We salute you, mothers of our land.

ONOLA   Our visitors must be hungry.
Look sharp, my daughters.
Let's prepare a feast fit for warriors
For our Princes.

[*Exit* SERVANTS.]

ONOLA   [*to* ABOAN] The Prince and Lady Imoinda
Have much to talk about. I suggest
We retire to another room and leave
Them to themselves.

[*Exit* LADY ONOLA *and* ABOAN.]

[*The attraction between* OROONOKO *and* PRINCESS
IMOINDA *is immediate and mutual.*]

IMOINDA   You must thank Lady Onola for me.
Since my father passed she
Has been my mother and father. All
Over the kingdom, whispers are
Forever flying around about her.
Lies mostly, spread by wretches
Envious of her success in the palm
Kernel trade. She has farms that stretch
Further than the eye can see, and over a
Thousand people working for her.
And she treats every one of them as
Though they were her very own children. You
Saw that yourself just then.

OROONOKO   [*nods*] Is it true what I've heard
That she once was the King's
Paramour?

IMOINDA   [*laughs*] It is true. But that was a
Long time ago, when she was

But a girl. The King sent her the Royal Veil
Of Invitation, which is customary,
When His Highness has a mind to
Honour a lady with his bed.
[*hurrying on*] As I said, that was
Long ago. She has freedom of
The palace still, the only man or woman,
Outside of royalty, that enjoys the privilege.
The King lets her. His advisers are scandalised.
I have heard her say the most outrageous
Things to his face. He merely
Laughs, saying that he wished only that all his
Ministers put together possessed half a nought
Of her nerve. She enjoys royal immunity.
But the King's councillors would get her if they
                    could.
She makes them uneasy.
Speaking of courage: how did my father
Die? What happened during his last moments
Of life?

OROONOKO   Your father was a great and valiant
General. His going was quick. After
The cowardly blow that felled him, he
Tarried along only long enough to
Speak about you.
This is what he said:
That you were
A child that must not be touched
By dew.
That you were
The light with which he found his way
On difficult journeys
And in seasons of darkness.
This is what he didn't say – and I
Wish he had, I wish he had –
That your smile
Rises like the sun on the misty
Wilderness of a warrior's life.

IMOINDA   [*mock frown*] It does?

OROONOKO   That your smile
           Is like the dawn going poaching
           In the dark orchard of this warrior's
           Sleep.
IMOINDA   [*smiling*] Is that so? My smile is now a thief?
OROONOKO   That the stars,
           Melted together, cooled in the sea,
           And cut into a stone brighter than
           The sun, are bright. But not half
           As bright as your smile.
IMOINDA   Are you being serious?
OROONOKO   I haven't been more serious in my life,
           Imoinda.
IMOINDA   I can see that, my Lord, I can see that.
           I don't know whether to run or to jump
           For joy.
OROONOKO   Your feet are set deep
           In the sea, home of the Goddess Oya,
           Who when she wakes up in time present,
           Her eyes heavy with dream, shakes her
           Head crowned with a nest of birds
           Baited into her trap with promise of fish.
           Escaping one by one, the birds carry
           Between their beaks greetings, hope, regrets
           And dreams from time past to time future.

           I am one of those birds, Imoinda.
           I have burrowed my past, a
           Bloodstained bundle wrapped in
           Seaweed, into the cleansing salt-water vaults
           Of the sea goddess. I wear time present
           Like a charm for luck.

           And the future that I am soaring
           Into is you, Imoinda.
           I have come
           To your feet, set deep in the sea,
           Home of the Goddess Oya
           Who alone knows the path

That leads into this world
And the road that guides
Us out of it.

Give me your ear, Imoinda, I
Have but one thing to say to you,
And it's the most important thing
I've said in my life:
Be with me.

> [*Enter* OROMBO, *unnoticed by* OROONOKO *and*
> PRINCESS IMOINDA. *He eavesdrops.*]

IMOINDA My Lord, Prince Oroonoko,
I do not know the secret of the sea,
Where it goes or from where it sets
Or if its fish are thoughts made flesh.
But I know this for I've seen it with my eyes:
That from it the sun rises in the morning
And into it it plunges at night.

I do not know the secret of rain,
How it shelters from the sun
Or whether its mistress is the ocean.
But I know this for I've seen it with my eyes:
Rain is the beard of God, rinsed in milk, the
Flag of being. No barber on earth possesses
The blade to shave it off.

I do not know the secret of the mirror,
Whether it sees the world or sees illusions
Or whether it sees a world filled with illusions.
But I know this for I've seen it with my eyes:
From this day till I'm ninety-nine or more.
Or till I die before making ninety-nine, I shall do up
My hair in the mirror of your eyes.

Be with me, Oroonoko.

> [*Exit* OROMBO *with a thoughtful smirk.*]

Scene 4

The Palace.

The KABIYESI *is on his throne. He has the glazed looked of deep drunkenness. He is bored to distraction.*

Enter OROMBO. *He has the urgent comportment of a man who has come with a message.*

Exit the ROYAL DRUMMERS *and* DANCERS, *dismissed by the* KABIYESI *with an almost imperceptible gesture.*

OROMBO   When others drink wine,
         You drink blood, my King.
         When others plant yams
         You're planting the heads
         Of men. When others reap
         Fruit, you're harvesting
         The breath of warriors.
         [*prostrates himself*] I am your most devoted
         Slave, my Warrior King.

KABIYESI   You waffle a lot, Orombo,
         But there's salt and pepper
         In your waffle.
         What is it this time?

OROMBO   I bring you news, Kabiyesi.
         I bring you tidings that will
         Make your heart sing, your
         Loins dance, and the seraglio
         Roar at your hunting skills.

KABIYESI   You have found me a maiden.

OROMBO   Not just any maiden, my King,
         But one that dwells at
         Heights unknown on the crest
         Of beauty –

KABIYESI   – Does this beauty have a name?

OROMBO   Her name, Kabiyesi, is baked
         In honey, coated in honey, and

To be relished like honey. Imoinda,
'The little honeyed one'. She
Comes with pedigree: her father
Was your very own Generalissimo,
The Akogun, our departed chief of warriors.

KABIYESI   I do remember her. She was but
A child when she last came to
Court.

OROMBO   She's bloomed, Kabiyesi,
She's bloomed into full-blown
Splendour. A purple star blown
Into our earth by the crack of
Lightning at dawn, Kabiyesi.

KABIYESI   [*heartily*] Orombo!

OROMBO   I mention the dawn, Kabiyesi, because
She is fresh like the dawn.
Her face is fresh, her hands are fresh,
Her bosom is fresh – discretion
Prevents me from naming all
Other parts of her that are
Fresh like the dawn, Kabiyesi.

KABIYESI   Go on, Orombo.

OROMBO   If you insist, Kabiyesi.
Her face is fresh, her bosom is fresh,
Even the swollen valleys between her
Thighs are fresh like the dawn.

KABIYESI   A virgin? And not spoken for?

OROMBO   Spoken for! Don't swear in
The presence of His Highness,
Your Highness! Spoken for!
How can she be spoken for,
When this very night His Highness
Will honour her with the Royal
Veil of Invitation? 'Spoken for',
Kabiyesi!

KABIYESI   All the same, has she no suitors?

OROMBO   The queue of noblemen knocking
At her door stretches from here to
Djenne and Timbuktu.

KABIYESI	And she has said no to every one of them?
OROMBO	She has said no to every one of them.
	She hands out 'no' to her suitors
	Like alms to beggars. She likes to
	Say no, Kabiyesi.
KABIYESI	You mean to say she's headstrong?
OROMBO	She likes to say no, Kabiyesi.
	That is all I am prepared to say.
KABIYESI	I like them headstrong.
	[*to a* PAGE] Slow, Painful Death!
SLOW, PAINFUL DEATH	Slow, Painful Death at your
	Service, my King.
KABIYESI	Fetch the Veil of Invitation.
SLOW, PAINFUL DEATH	Right away, my King.

[*Exit* SLOW, PAINFUL DEATH.]

KABIYESI	You know I like them headstrong,
	Orombo.
OROMBO	I am but your slave, Kabiyesi,
	I dare not presume. I merely
	Anticipate.

Scene 5

A room in LADY ONOLA's *household. It is raining outside.*

Enter OROONOKO *and* LADY ONOLA.

OROONOKO	I hope you don't mind
	The suddenness of it all.
ONOLA	Affairs of the heart are never
	Too sudden.
OROONOKO	Thank you, Lady Onola.
	I'd be most grateful if the
	News didn't go beyond this
	House until I've had the
	Chance to tell the King.
ONOLA	Your secret is safe in my house.
OROONOKO	He'll be thrilled by the news.
ONOLA	I'm sure he will.

[*Lightning captures them in a snapshot. Thunder.*]

ONOLA That girl is like a daughter to me.

OROONOKO I know.

ONOLA I'm like a mother to her.

OROONOKO I know, Lady Onola.

ONOLA Of all the women of our mighty
Kingdom, Prince Oroonoko, from
Those that dwell in the gaze of the palace
To those that dwell in the shade of the hills –

The wives-to-be and the newly married brides.
The maids with burnished marks
On their cheeks – those caramel stripes
That enhance their beauty still.
The ones with radiant gaps in their teeth
– An emblem of beauty, gifted by the Gods –
The elegant ones: the ones for whom a prince
May lust, the ones for whom a slave revolts.
The ones with childbearing hips.
The ones with hips that spark unrest in
The loins of happily married men.
The ones that glow like the pearls on their neck.
The ones with the grace of a lounging cat.

– Take them one and all together,
Ask them all bar none together,
And you'll find, Prince Oroonoko, that
None is as happy as my daughter is
Tonight. And fewer even still, as happy
As I am for the both of you.

OROONOKO Thank you, Lady Onola. My
Happiness knows no bounds.

ONOLA I do not question your honour.

OROONOKO I'm sure, Lady Onola.

ONOLA Nor would I for a moment doubt your
Word.

OROONOKO [*now not quite so sure*] I'm sure, Lady Onola.

ONOLA   I am just a woman who
Likes to speak her mind:
I know that many a time, on your
Numerous campaigns, in the course
Of your distinguished career, you have
Deflected from your side the arrow tipped with
Pestilent poison; the spear that quarters
An elephant's flesh; the white man's brutal
Burning beans that spread like smallpox
Through the air.

OROONOKO   Luck has been on my side, Lady Onola,
The Gods have been kind to me.

ONOLA   May they continue to do so, Prince
Oroonoko. But all those scourges will be nothing,
Nothing! Compared to the boundless bane
Of my bitterness should you ever break my
Daughter's heart. You would wake
Up on that day and find that your dreams
Have turned into a rising pillar of dust.
Do we understand each other – ?

OROONOKO   [*stunned*] – Only too well –

ONOLA   – My Lord and warrior?

OROONOKO   – Lady Onola.

ONOLA   [*smiles.*] Don't look so hurt.

OROONOKO   Me, hurt? The very thought of it!

[*He looks very, very hurt.*]

ONOLA   [*laughs.*] I'm glad we've got that out of the
Way. We can now go back and join
The others. We must discuss
The wedding.

OROONOKO   The *wedding?*

ONOLA   Yes. It would be a shame if all the troubles
I went through this past week; the rams
I bought, the countless kegs of wine I
Ordered, the sacks of yam, the tons of
Fish, the musicians I hired –

OROONOKO	[*trembling*] Wait, wait. You – you have been preparing *What* for a week?
ONOLA	The wedding.
OROONOKO	*My* wedding?
ONOLA	Yes. I hope you don't mind.
OROONOKO	I don't understand any of this, Lady Onola. The Princess and I met only Tonight.
ONOLA	I knew, long before you arrived, that You were meant for her and she For you. Call it an older woman's Intuition. Upon my honour, Prince Oroonoko, The Princess knew nothing of my designs.
OROONOKO	[*all too casually*] Have you set the date?
ONOLA	You're free tonight, Aren't you?
OROONOKO	Yes, I'm – [*in disbelief*] Tonight? Did you say tonight?
ONOLA	Yes.
OROONOKO	But there's protocol, Lady Onola. I have to inform the King.
ONOLA	Protocol allows also for the King To be *pleasantly* surprised.
OROONOKO	Why the haste?
ONOLA	Trust me, Prince Oroonoko, I'll Explain to you when I have A moment to spare. But not now –
OROONOKO	No, Lady Onola. I demand an Explanation. Now.

[*Enter a servant of the King,* SLOW. PAINFUL DEATH.
He is soaked to the skin.]

ONOLA	Here comes your explanation.
SLOW. PAINFUL DEATH	Evening, Lady Onola. I bring a message for Princess Imoinda.
ONOLA	Give it to me. I'll pass it on.

SLOW. PAINFUL DEATH   [*haughtily*] I'm sorry, Lady Onola, but
        It is a matter strictly between
        The palace and the Princess.

ONOLA   In that case, sir, go back and tell
        The palace that I swept away
        Your feet from the threshold
        Of my house. Tell the palace that I
        Used a broom. If I see you
        Here again, I shall use a
        Lash or worse.

SLOW. PAINFUL DEATH   [*loses his temper, shouts*]
        Do you know who I am?

ONOLA   [*to* OROONOKO] The poor man doesn't know
        Who he is. Can you help him?

SLOW. PAINFUL DEATH   I am a servant of the King,
        You hear! A servant of the King!
        [*gives up, pleads*] I'm only doing my job,
        Lady Onola. You know
        I bear you no ill will.

ONOLA   I suppose I should be grateful
        For that. Now, leave.

SLOW. PAINFUL DEATH   You know what will happen to me,
        If I go back to the palace
        Without delivering this errand –

ONOLA   I have no pity to waste on you.
        You're spineless. You have no
        Manners – and, I didn't quite
        Catch your name.

SLOW. PAINFUL DEATH   They'd kill me, Lady Onola, you
        Know they'd kill me! I beg you,
        Lady Onola, please, let me
        See Princess Imoinda.

[LADY ONOLA *does not budge.*]

SLOW. PAINFUL DEATH   [*sighs*] You didn't hear it from me:
        His Highness – long may he reign – has
        Decided to honour Princess Imoinda
        With the Royal Veil of Invitation.

OROONOKO   The Royal Veil of Invitation!

ONOLA   [*with a 'you see?' look at* OROONOKO] Leave this to me.
[*to* SLOW, PAINFUL DEATH]
Why are you so drenched, O servant
Of our King?

SLOW, PAINFUL DEATH   [*confused and irritable*]
It's raining, you can see that it's raining.

ONOLA   Was it raining when you left the palace?

SLOW, PAINFUL DEATH   No, it wasn't.
But as I stepped outside the main gates
A great wind struck me in the face.
I looked up into the sky and saw
A flaming brand with dark
Wisps high above the towering
Cliffs of cloud. Flashes of lightning gave
Way to booming thunder. Ahead of me
The earth shook with shrieking sounds.
The wind collided with whirling dust.
They heaved and twisted like wrestlers.
The storm came swiftly. The rain, roaring
Like a great beast, began to pour.
I was frightened, Lady Onola. I'm not
Ashamed to admit to you that I was frightened.
Out there, as we speak, Lady Onola, the wells are
Filled to the brim, the creeks are
Overflowing, valleys are welling
With water, trees felled by the wind,
Thickets squashed. I saw an entire compound
Bounding away on a rush of floodwater,
Like a boat caught in roiling rapids. The
World is a frightening place tonight, Lady Onola,
People are dying out there.

ONOLA   Have you wife or children?

SLOW, PAINFUL DEATH   None.

ONOLA   Good. The matter between us is
Simple. You want to keep your
Head and body together.
I want to keep the King
Away from my daughter –

SLOW. PAINFUL DEATH   [*prostrating himself, in tears*]
                Please, Lady Onola –
        ONOLA Hear me out. You say that
                You bear no ill thoughts towards me.
                I wish you no evil either. This is what
                I propose we do: you will
                Shelter here tonight or until
                The storm abates. I shall arrange for
                You to be ferried out of town
                And on to some place else
                Where you can settle down, with
                Three bags of cowries or more to your
                Name, and start your life anew.
SLOW. PAINFUL DEATH   But, Lady Onola! His Highness will
                Declare a bounty on my head.
        ONOLA He will do no such thing.
                How is he to know that you were not
                Swept away by that great storm out there?
SLOW. PAINFUL DEATH   [*despondently*]
                Very well, Lady Onola, I shall do
                As you say.
        ONOLA Follow your right hand. The guest
                House is there.
SLOW. PAINFUL DEATH   [*in a daze*] Lady Onola?
        ONOLA Yes?
SLOW. PAINFUL DEATH   Did you say bags?
        ONOLA I did.
SLOW. PAINFUL DEATH   Did you say cowries?
        ONOLA I did.
SLOW. PAINFUL DEATH   Did you say bags and cowries together?
        ONOLA I did.
SLOW. PAINFUL DEATH   Did you say three?
        ONOLA I did.
SLOW. PAINFUL DEATH   Did you say three bags of cowries?
        ONOLA Yes. But of course if that's not enough –
SLOW. PAINFUL DEATH   God bless you, Lady Onola.
                [*tearfully, joyously*] I'm rich. I'm rich. God bless
                You, Lady Onola.

[*Exit* SLOW. PAINFUL DEATH.]

OROONOKO How did you know that
That would happen? That
My grandfather would send the
Veil of Invitation?

[*Enter* SLOW. PAINFUL DEATH, *looking lost.*]

ONOLA I said follow your right hand.
Your right hand is the other way.
SLOW. PAINFUL DEATH   I'm rich. I'm rich. God bless
You, Lady Onola. The world
Is a wonderful place.

[*Exit* SLOW. PAINFUL DEATH.]

ONOLA I know the King and his minions.
I know the workings of their minds.
OROONOKO I'm clearly out of my depth.
ONOLA You've been away far too long from
The court, my warrior. You'll learn,
My Prince, you'll learn soon enough.
But it won't be long now before we can
Breathe easily again. Tradition forbids
The King to go near his grandson's bride.
Come on, child, there's no time
To waste. Every moment wasted is
Another arrow added to the enemy's
Quiver.

[*Exit* LADY ONOLA *and* OROONOKO.]

Scene 6

The Palace.

Enter OROMBO, *wet.*

The KABIYESI, *fallen into a light sleep, stirs.*

OROMBO Still no sign of him, Your Highness.

KABIYESI Perhaps it's the storm?

OROMBO [*doubtfully*] Perhaps.

KABIYESI Perhaps he's stopped for shelter.

OROMBO Perhaps. But he would not do that,
Your Highness. He knows not
To do that. I observed him carefully
When he left. He had the
Look of a man with burning
Ambitions to live long enough
To see tomorrow.

[*He paces restlessly about. then comes to a sudden, decisive halt.*]

OROMBO Red, Dark Death, warrior!

[RED, DARK DEATH *comes forward.*]

OROMBO Slow, Burning Death, warrior!

[SLOW, BURNING DEATH *comes forward.*]

OROMBO Swift, Violent Death, warrior!

[SWIFT, VIOLENT DEATH *comes forward.*]

OROMBO Sly, Sudden Death, warrior!

[SLY, SUDDEN DEATH *comes forward.*]

OROMBO Savage, Brutal Death, warrior!

[SAVAGE, BRUTAL DEATH *comes forward.*]

OROMBO Blue, Numbing Death, warrior!
Blue, Numbing Death, warrior!

SAVAGE, BRUTAL DEATH Blue, Numbing Death's off sick today,
Kabiyesi.
Down with the fever, my Chief.

OROMBO [*curtseys to the* KABIYESI] Follow me, all of you.
Here we come, Lady Onola.

[*Exit* OROMBO *and* GUARDS.]

Scene 7

A spacious hall in LADY ONOLA*'s house.*

The storm outside has ceased.

LADY ONOLA *and the other* WOMEN *as well as* DRUMMERS *and* MUSICIANS
are gathered for the wedding.

Enter OROONOKO, *accompanied by* ABOAN. OROONOKO *is holding a torch.*
He approaches PRINCESS IMOINDA *and hands her the torch.*

OROONOKO Take this flame. I will marry you.
            If anyone objects, burn their house.

            [*The* DRUMMERS *beat out a song of applause.*]

IMOINDA [*all smiles*] Those standing – let them stand well.
            Those stooping – let them stoop well.
            Those sitting outside on the veranda –
            Let them receive our thanks.
            Those who tried to but couldn't make
            It here – we do understand.
            You the elders, who have braved the storm,
            I thank you for honouring this day.

            I pounded yam softly,
            And offered it to Eshu, the trickster-God,
            The God of fate. Eshu refused to eat.
            Then I asked him:
            'Will you stay indoors or outside?'
            He said:
ALL   'Outside.'
IMOINDA When Death comes looking for me –
ALL   It will meet Eshu outside.
IMOINDA When Illness comes looking for me –
ALL   It will meet Eshu outside.
IMOINDA When Poverty comes looking for me –
ALL   It will meet Eshu outside.
IMOINDA When Evil comes looking for me –
ALL   It will meet Eshu outside.

IMOINDA But if a child comes looking for me –
    ALL Eshu will bring him in to your room.
IMOINDA If Laughter comes looking for me –
    ALL Eshu will show him in.
IMOINDA If Good Fortune comes looking for me –
    ALL Eshu will tell her to knock on your door.
IMOINDA You people of the world,
         Help me to thank my mother,
         For she decked me out in clothes
         Rich enough to make Oya,
         The sea-goddess, envious.

         Let everybody thank my mother:
         She did not allow me to borrow dresses
         From those who would turn round and abuse me.
         She dressed me in clothes so rich
         I could confuse a god.

         And you my parent, Lady Onola:
         When you don't see waves
         Will you forget the sea?
         When you don't see the lightning
         Will you forget the rain?
         When you don't see me any more
         Will you forget me?

         It was you who decided
         That I was old enough
         To move to another house.
         Don't leave me alone in that place.

         I look right, and left,
         I look behind and in front of me,
         But I see nobody
         Who resembles my other parents,
         The ones who birthed me.
         What kind of god created me
         In a sickly world

To make my mother die like rotten yam?
What kind of god created me
In a violent world
To make my father die in war?

If luck is not against me
I shall have them back with me
In my husband's house.
If luck is not against me
They shall re-enter the world
Through me.
My head – which is wearing a
Bright scarf today –
Will surely give me
Male children and female children.

I honour the bitter kola nut
For through it I shall gain Shango's favour.
I honour the red kola nut
For through it I will gain the favour of the other gods.
I honour the hot pepper
For it cures sickness.

The melon seed soup only offends the hungry man
Who was not invited to the feast.
The aroma of fried plantain only offends the hungry man
Who was not invited to the feast.

My people, mothers and fathers:
Today is a glorious day!

> [*Applause, music, dancing.*]

> [*The* GUESTS, *especially the men, launch into a comical song in which individuals improvise alternate lines in response to the chorus lines.*]

ALL [*singing*] Oroonoko's friends came in a band of three.
The threesome came wheezing with glee.

I'll swim across the river,
He said, to the third.
And I'll fight the weever,
He said, to the third.
I'll run against the drift,
He said, to the third,
Just to lie atop your gift,
He said, to her.

Oroonoko's friends came in a band of three.
The threesome came wheezing with glee.

His good first friend offered him tripe.
His great second friend offered him a pipe.
His best third friend offered him her breast.
Not once did he blink, he accepted with zest.
Not once did he blink, he went for her breast.

Oroonoko's friends came in a band of three.
The threesome came wheezing with glee.

I'll swim across the river,
He said, to the third.
And I'll fight the weever,
He said, to the third.
I'll run against the drift,
He said, to the third.
Just to lie atop your gift,
He said, to her.

> [*Enter* OROMBO *with his* 'WARRIORS'. *They have their bows at the ready with arrows.*]

OROMBO I see you're already celebrating
Ahead of the great news.

> [*He pulls out the Veil of Invitation and places it round* PRINCESS IMOINDA*'s neck but she shrugs it off.* OROMBO *does not bother to pick it up.*]

OROMBO May I congratulate you, Princess Imoinda
        On this most special occasion of your
        Inauguration as the King's a hundred and
        Fifty-eighth consort.

> [OROONOKO *moves threateningly towards* OROMBO.
> ABOAN *holds him back.*]

ONOLA   Welcome to my home, Chief Orombo.
        Do make yourself comfortable. Wine?
        Food? Please help yourself to anything
        That catches your fancy. As you can see,
        We are celebrating a great and joyous
        Occasion – the coming together in sacred
        Matrimony of our Prince and his
        Princess. We meant to invite
        The King. We meant to invite you too.
        But what with the storm, and youthful
        Impatience – and who can blame our Prince
        And Princess? – we were unable to do so.
        As you can see – and we all of us here can testify,
        They are now man and wife –

OROMBO Let me stop you before you go any
        Further. He may be her man but she's not
        His wife. The Prince cannot be wed
        Without the King's say-so.
        It is the law of the land, passed on to us
        By our fathers.

ONOLA   That is a lie, Chief Orombo. You know
        It's a lie.

OROMBO It is in my nature to lie, Lady Onola.
        It comes with the job.
        But I lie, remember, on the King's behalf.
        And the King does not lie. The King
        Cannot lie. It is theologically impossible for the
        King to lie. Therefore, in my capacity as Special
        Envoy to the King – or, if you like, the King's Chief
        Liar – and for the reasons stated above, etcetera, etcetera,
        I declare this marriage illegitimate and void.

IMOINDA   But you can't!

OROMBO   Oh yes I can. Watch me, I'm a wizard. On a
Good day I can even predict that tomorrow
Will surely follow from today. Usually, I'm right.
When you're ready, Princess Imoinda, the King's
Bedroom awaits your sumptuous presence.

OROONOKO [*being held back*] I'll kill him! I'll kill him!

OROMBO   You're a warrior, Prince Oroonoko. It
Is in your nature to kill. I sympathise with
You. But I am the King's slave, and there's the rub:
Unless His Highness decrees to the contrary,
My neck and body remain together. There's nothing
I can do about it, I'm afraid. It's the law of the land.

ONOLA   Tell the King who sent you here
That the sky will light up with stars once more.
Tell him that soon, on a night like this,
A million fireflies will be seen,
And the luminous half-disc of the moon
Will be sent by God to watch over us.

Tell him that the sun will spread across the land
That had been laid dank by the floods.
Tell him that the farms will suffer no more
And crops now drowning will be nursed back to life.

Tell him that rocks of mist will rise from the ground
And the glut of water that has surged into many homes
And taken many lives will be scooped up by the sun and
Poured back into the sky.
Tell him that among the creatures
That have survived the flood there will be mothers in milk.

Tell the King who sent you here
That prayer is the bounty of God
And that the King like God
Must know this truth:
That life is a whip that strikes
The strong and the weak alike.

Tell him that life is a journey.
And that no matter how large
A forest may be, there is a town
At the end of it. And if there's
Not town, there's the sea. And
If there's not sea, there's the
Desert. And no matter how
Large that desert may be,
There's a town at the end of it.

OROMBO I love it when you're angry,
You speak such cultivated nonsense.
Pity you're not my wife. I'd knock
That rubbish right out of your head
With an onslaught of semen that'd
Hit you like a wild storm.

ONOLA Dream on, Orombo.
Go with them, my daughter.
The King is a neutered dog
On heat. I should apologise to dogs on heat.
He's impotent. You have nothing to
Fear from him.

OROMBO The King is the King, Lady Onola.
If you say that again, I shall
Be very angry with you.

ONOLA I said the King cannot perform.
Is that another theological
Impossibility?

OROMBO Keep theology out of this.
The King is well equipped.
You'll have to excuse me, fellow
Citizens, good people. Duty calls.
[*bends down and picks up the Veil of Invitation*]
Let the feast continue, indulge yourselves
On the King's behalf.

[*Exit* OROMBO *with* PRINCESS IMOINDA *his captive.*]

Act Three

Scene 1

LADY ONOLA's *house: later that night.*

The party has dispersed and OROONOKO *is alone.*

Enter ABOAN.

OROONOKO	Any news?
ABOAN	We followed them right
	Up till the palace gates.
	But the guards wouldn't let
	Us inside.
OROONOKO	Didn't they know you? Didn't you
	Tell them that I sent you to the King?
ABOAN	They would not be swayed.
OROONOKO	How was the Princess?
ABOAN	She held her head high.
	[*swallows*] She wept all the way.
	[*beside himself with fury*] Things cannot go on like this.
	Orombo is destroying Coramantien. The King
	Listens to him alone. His other advisers
	Are dead, exiled or too scared
	Of Orombo to speak their mind. Orombo
	Is dangerous, my General. Anyone can see
	From a week's trek off, that his sight is
	Set on the throne. We must do something about
	Him.
OROONOKO	Are you suggesting, Aboan, that we
	Rise against the King?
ABOAN	I suggest no such thing, Prince Oroonoko.
	All I'm saying is, Orombo is a scourge.
OROONOKO	He happens also to be the King's Chief
	Adviser. Any deed against him is a deed
	Against the King. It's called treason,
	Aboan. I'll hear no more of it.

[handwritten annotation: Conflict of duty]

ABOAN   With all respect, my General:
You're making an error
We may not live to regret.

OROONOKO   You threaten me if you threaten
The King, Aboan. Are you threatening the
King, *warrior?*

ABOAN   [*gives up*] No, my General. I've overstepped the
Bounds. Forgive me.

OROONOKO   Can't you see, Aboan, that Orombo
Was right? I had no business doing
What I did tonight without the King's
Express permission. It was foolish of
Me, and childish. You, Aboan,
Should have advised me against it.

ABOAN   I did too, my General. You enjoined
Me to share my counsel with the breeze.

OROONOKO   I'd had too much wine to drink.
You should have tried harder.

ABOAN   I shall not fail to do so next time.

OROONOKO   If there is a next time.
At the rise of dawn, I shall
Go to the palace and throw
Myself at the mercy of the King.
My behaviour tonight was unbecoming
Of a man in my position. I expect him
To ask for my head.

ABOAN   I am to blame, sir. Let me go
With you before the King and
Let him know that the blame is
Mine.

OROONOKO   Your words are kind, Aboan, and
I value your friendship. But you know
This as well as I do, that the tree that
Falls in the forest does not kill people
In the house. The roof that crashes down
In the back room does not kill people on
The street. We were not born together, my
Dear friend, why should we die together?

ABOAN   You flatter me when you call me your
             Friend, my Lord. You know as well
             As I do that you're my master
             And I'm your slave. I shall go with
             You before the King.

[*Enter* LADY ONOLA.]

ONOLA   I've come straight from the palace,
             Prince Oroonoko –

OROONOKO   [*to* ABOAN] Tell this woman that I do not
             Wish to speak to her.

[*Exit* OROONOKO.]

Scene 2

The Palace. The Royal Bath.

Music wafts like incense across the room.

The KABIYESI *is sat naked in a resplendent marble bath enjoying a massage from the hands of a* EUNUCH. *The* KABIYESI *frequently picks up a mirror and admires himself.*

Enter PRINCESS IMOINDA, *led in by* GUARDS.

IMOINDA   [*in tears*] We've been taught, Kabiyesi, that you're
             Like the ripe coconut that falls on a child
             At night.

             If a man greets you, there is trouble.
             If a man forgets to greet you, there is trouble.

             Our fathers say that anyone
             Who shakes a tree trunk
             Succeeds only in shaking himself.

             I do not resist you, my King.
             The seeds of the ayo board game
             Do not complain about being shoved about.
             You kill your enemies gently like the leopard
             – When it kills, its tail rests gently on the ground.

> Do not smile at me, my Lord,
> Your smile frightens me.
> Whenever you open your mouth
> You swallow a hero –

KABIYESI Enough of that, my dear, take off
That lovely dress and join us in
This fabulous bath. Come in and
Swallow a hero.

[*The* EUNUCH *forces back a giggle.*]

IMOINDA My King –
KABIYESI Yes?
IMOINDA I'm married.
KABIYESI So am I.
[*laughs*] I've been told that you like
To say no. I on the other hand
Have always been deaf to the
Sound of no. It's a congenital
Affliction, you see, no always
Sounds like yes to my ears. I
Tend to take a no and yes it up.
Come in, lovely girl, don't begrudge
An old man of those ripe delectable
Bosoms.

[*Slowly, silently,* PRINCESS IMOINDA *takes off her clothes one by one until she is stark naked. She gets into the bath. The* KABIYESI *places her hand on his crotch.*]

KABIYESI There's no need to be coy, my dear,
It's your very own plaything
Tonight.
IMOINDA [*wearily*] I don't think it wants to be disturbed.
KABIYESI [*irritably*] Only a shut-eye, my dear, only
A short nap.
[*reaches for her head*] Perhaps it sulks. Let's see what
It does when you bid it welcome.

[*He pushes her head down between his legs.* PRINCESS

[IMOINDA *stays there for several seconds. Then she raises her head, choking, gasping for breath. The* KABIYESI *pushes her down once more. Once more, she chokes and gasps for breath. On a reflex she reaches for the mirror lying by the side of the bath. In one swift movement of her wrist she brings it slashing down between the* KABIYESI's *legs. There is a long silence. The bath water turns red. The* EUNUCH *starts screaming. The* KABIYESI *flies out of the bath, limping around in agony. Blood flows freely from his crotch.* PRINCESS IMOINDA *is in a state of shock.*]

[*Enter* OROMBO.]

[*The* GUARDS *rush to cover* KABIYESI *with a gown and tend to his wound.*]

KABIYESI [*as he is carried off*] Hang that witch! Hang Her!

[*Exit the* KABIYESI.]

[OROMBO *smiles broadly.*]

OROMBO [*to the* GUARDS] Let's show her how real men do it.

[*He lowers his trousers.*]

Scene 3

LADY ONOLA's *house.*

OROONOKO *is on his feet, fast asleep.*

A sharp knock on the door.

Enter ABOAN, *agitated.*

OROONOKO *draws his sword, startled out of his slumber.*

ABOAN It's only me, my General.
OROONOKO Learn to knock.
ABOAN Something terrible has happened
At the palace.

OROONOKO   What?
ABOAN   No one knows why but
           The King has decreed that the Princess
           Must die.
OROONOKO   [*warily*] And why would His Highness do such a thing?
ABOAN   Nobody knows.
OROONOKO   Let's go.

                    [*He stumbles.*]

ABOAN   [*anxiously*] Oroonoko!
OROONOKO   [*steadies himself*] Let's go, warrior.

                    [*Exit* OROONOKO *and* ABOAN.]

                        Scene 4

The slave port.

Enter OROMBO, *followed by* PRINCESS IMOINDA *in chains and led in by the* GUARDS. *She is all bloodied up and can hardly walk.*

OROMBO   Consider yourself lucky
           That I decided to commute
           Your sentence to this. You didn't
           Know that I had it in me to be
           Compassionate, did you? Well,
           I am that sort of man. Hard on
           The surface, soft as a whispered
           Sigh on the inside.

                    [*Enter* CAPTAIN STANMORE, *looking not a little irritated. He is followed in by several of his* CREW, *all like himself, European. They are armed with shotguns and pistols.*]

                    [CAPTAIN STANMORE *examines* PRINCESS IMOINDA.]

STANMORE   Is this why you had to disturb my
           Sleep?
OROMBO   She's a princess, you see. The King
           Wanted her dead. I had to bring her
           At once.

STANMORE	How much?
OROMBO	The usual.
STANMORE	Out of the question.
OROMBO	Less five percent.
STANMORE	She's all swollen.
OROMBO	Less ten percent.
STANMORE	She hardly can walk.
OROMBO	Fifteen.
STANMORE	She looks half dead.
OROMBO	Twenty.
STANMORE	And five.
	Five and twenty.
OROMBO	Done. Give her a good scrub – nothing fancy,
	Some porous rocks will do the trick.
	And she'll be as good as new.
IMOINDA	Do as the King commanded. Kill me.
OROMBO	[*ignores her*] Kabiyesi was involved in an accident
	Earlier tonight. It is unlikely he'll recover.
	If he passes, as I'm sure he will, I intend to
	Be first in line for that lovely little trophy that's
	Called the throne. In order to do so as smoothly
	As possible, I intend to round up this woman's
	So-called husband and all his men. His name
	Is Oroonoko. He harbours ambitions of succeeding
	The King. He is a dangerous character.
STANMORE	I don't quite catch your drift.
OROMBO	What I'm saying, Captain Stanley, is that
	There is a lot more waiting where this wench
	Came from. What I'm saying, Captain Stanley,
	Is that you can have them all for half the going rate.
	All I ask of you – you and your men – is that you help
	My men and I bring them to heel. Scratch my back,
	I scratch yours, I'm that sort of man.
STANMORE	[*thoughtfully*] So I've heard. I happen
	To know Captain Green.
OROMBO	How's my friend Captain Brown?
STANMORE	Green. His name is Green.
	Cursing your very name.

| | Half the men he bought from
| | You have dived into the sea.
| OROMBO | I did tell him they were warriors.
| | They either kill or die.
| IMOINDA | Jingling horseman, fast traveller
| | Who settles his quarrels with a spear,
| | The road is clouded in dust
| | When you pursue your enemy.
| STANMORE | What's the girl saying?
| OROMBO | Don't mind her, she's praying to
| | Soponna, the God of the pox.
| STANMORE | [*steps back*] Has she the plague?
| OROMBO | No need to be alarmed, Captain
| | Stanley –
| STANMORE | *More.* Stanmore.
| OROMBO | Don't be alarmed, Captain More Stanmore.
| | She hasn't got the plague. She's merely
| | Praying for death. Why don't you and
| | Your men retire to the boat and discuss
| | My little proposal?
| STANMORE | Wait here.

[*Exit* CAPTAIN STANMORE *and his* MEN.]

| IMOINDA | Jingling horseman in a cloud of sand,
| | In the wake of your visit
| | Many fall asleep
| | Who will never wake up.

Spare me, O horseman, and spare my
Household too. But if you want to carry
My load, horseman. If my time has come
To go, horseman. Let me follow you to
Your home, horseman.

Jingling horseman in a mist of sand,
Carry me to your home beyond the trail of dust.
Hold me, heavenly tormentor,
Hold me in your arm.

[*She tries to strangle herself.* OROMBO *strikes her.*]

OROMBO It's fine by me if you want to
Kill yourself. But have the decency
To wait until the white man has paid
For you.

Scene 5

The Palace.

The KABIYESI *has died. His freshly deceased body, covered, is carried in by a couple of* PAGES.

Enter OROONOKO, ABOAN *and* LADY ONOLA.

OROONOKO [*taking in the situation*] When did it happen?
1ST ROYAL DRUMMER   Soon after the first cockcrow, my Lord.
OROONOKO Send out the town crier.
TOWN CRIER The King is dead! Long live the King!

[*Exit* TOWN CRIER.]

OROONOKO Call a meeting of the council of elders.
Can anyone tell me where the Princess's
Hanging was meant to take place?
TOWN CRIER [*off*] The King is dead! Long live the King!
1ST ROYAL DRUMMER Your Highness – long may you reign –
Princess Imoinda will not be hanged.
I overheard Chief Orombo talking
To his men –
ROYAL DRUMMERS [*all*] He mentioned the port.
ONOLA [*gasps*] They've gone to sell her.
OROONOKO The horses, Aboan. Saddle the horses.
Rally the men together.
TOWN CRIER [*off*] The King is dead! Long live the King!

[*Exit* ABOAN.]

OROONOKO [*to* LADY ONOLA] I pray you forgive me,
Lady Onola.
ONOLA [*smiles, sadly*] I have forgiven you. Hurry now
And fetch me my daughter.

[*Exit* OROONOKO *and* ALL *except* LADY ONOLA.]

ONOLA   Don't let me down, Ogun.
            Don't let me down.
            [*falls on her knees and weeps*]
            Bring me back my daughter, Ogun.
            You know she's the only one
            I've got.
TOWN CRIER [*off*] The King is dead! Long live the King!

            [*Exit* LADY ONOLA.]

                          Scene 6

The slave port.

OROMBO *is addressing his* MEN. *He is bitterness personified.*

OROMBO   You all heard what the white man
            Said. He does not want to get involved.
            That's all the thanks I get for these many
            Years of loyalty and honest trade with
            Him. He does not want to get involved!
            All I asked of him was a few men with
            Those nifty fire-spitting metals that
            Go 'shakaboola'! And a man is dead.
            That was all I asked. But what does
            He say? He does not want to get
            Involved, that's what he says.
            You all know what that means, don't you?
            It means that we're in serious trouble
            If the King dies. It means that we're in hot
            Pepper with that witch Onola
            And her twin-devil Oroonoko. If the
            King dies, those two will use our
            Scalps to drink palm-wine. We must
            Get back to the palace now, and be
            Ready to flee if the King's
            Condition worsens. If he

Makes it till noon, that
May give us time to summon some
Help.

[*Enter* OROONOKO, ABOAN *and other* WARRIORS.]

OROMBO [*to* OROONOKO] She's dead, my General.
OROONOKO [*simultaneously*] Where's she?
OROMBO Gone, my Lord. The King –
OROONOKO I know His Highness – may he rest
In peace – ordered her death –
OROMBO Kabiyesi is dead?

[*He weeps.*]

ABOAN The King is not dead, you scavenger.
You stand before the King.
OROMBO [*prostrates himself*] Long may you reign, my King.

[ABOAN *kicks him.*]

ABOAN Where's the Princess?
OROMBO She's now with our ancestors. After the King,
May He Rest, ordered that
She was hanged, I took pity on her,
And brought her here –
ABOAN You took pity on her and brought her *here*?
OROMBO She died from her own hands
As we waited for the white man to
Come down from his boat.
OROONOKO [*grief-stricken*] Her body?
OROMBO She rests in the water.
ABOAN [*benumbed*] The Princess died and you
Dumped her in the sea?

[*He pulls out a dagger.*]

ABOAN [*to* OROONOKO] Your Highness – long may you
Reign – have I your permission
To slaughter him like a dog?
OROONOKO Make it slow and painful.
OROMBO [*deliberately*] You'll be pleased to know that
She didn't die a virgin. I saw to it.

[OROONOKO *pulls out a dagger and pounces on* OROMBO *all in the same moment.* OROMBO *dies spluttering blood. His* MEN *watch, huddled together, terrified.*]

OROONOKO   Kill them.
No, take them back to the palace.
Feed them to the crocodiles.

[*Enter* CAPTAIN STANMORE *and his* MEN.]

STANMORE   I changed my mind.

[*He sees* OROMBO's *body.*]

STANMORE   [*in mock sorrow*] Oh no.

[*One of the* WARRIORS *makes to attack* CAPTAIN STANMORE *but is brought down in a hail of bullets.*]

STANMORE   So, which one of you is the
Great pretender to the throne
Of Coramantien?
OROONOKO   [*formally*] I am Prince Oroonoko,
Commander-in-Chief of the gallant
Warriors of Coramantien.
You are – ?
STANMORE   [*shakes* OROONOKO's *hand*] Captain James Stanmore,
Prince Oroonoko –
May I call you Bob?
OROONOKO   You may not.
STANMORE   From this moment onwards,
And until it pleases me to dispose
Of you in a manner that I deem fit,
You are my cargo, my slave.
That means, alas, Your Highness –
I'll spell it out – that I am
Your lord and master. And
Your name, *Prince* Oroonoko,
Is Bob.

[*Slow fade to black.*]

PART TWO

SURINAM

Act One

Scene 1

A portside slave-hold in Surinam: several months later.

Enter MR TREFRY *and* DEPUTY GOVERNOR BYAM.

We can hear a nearly inaudible welter of voices singing a slow lament in the distance.

TREFRY	Well, Byam, Captain Stanmore Has brought us a fresh supply.
BYAM	Aye, and I'm sure we've never had More need of them.
TREFRY	And I'm afraid we shall never have Less.
BYAM	What do you say, Trefry?
TREFRY	We shall have enough of them, I Warrant you, when they come to breed.
BYAM	Breed! They are lazy, obstinate and unruly pagans – Half of them are so sulky when they arrive That a Christian may beat them till he drops Before he can make them to eat, if they Haven't a mind to it. He may beat those that will eat, long enough Before they will work. And what with their Starving themselves, they die as fast As flies and the poor industrious planter Loses the money they cost him, and his ground Runs to ruin for want of their labour. A Christian colony has a hard time of it, That is forced to deal in this heathen commodity. Every time a ship comes in, my money Goes for a great raw-boned Negro fellow That has the impudence to think he Is my fellow creature, with as much right

To Liberty as I have, and so grows sullen
And refuses to work; or for a young wench
Who will howl night and day after a brat or
A lover, which nothing can drive out of her
Head but a cat-o'-nine-tails. And if recourse
Is had to that remedy, it's ten to one that
She'll take the next opportunity to pick
My pocket by hanging herself.
The women are worse than the men.

[*Exit* BYAM.]

[*Enter* CAPTAIN STANMORE.]

STANMORE   Mr Trefry.
TREFRY   Captain Stanmore.
STANMORE   How fares our illustrious
Deputy Governor, Mr Byam?
TREFRY   Somewhat out of sorts.
STANMORE   In love still?
TREFRY   Captain?
STANMORE   I hear the Deputy Governor has taken
A fancy to one of the female slaves
And yet, would you believe, she gives herself
Airs and will scarcely speak to him. What do
They call her – Clemene?
TREFRY   She was in a lot that I drew for the
Lord Governor.
STANMORE   The Lord Governor? And when do we
Expect his Lordship's return from England?
TREFRY   Any day now.

[*Enter* BYAM.]

BYAM   [*to* TREFRY] There's no resisting your fortune, Trefry.
You draw all the prizes.
TREFRY   I draw for our Lord Governor, you know;
His fortune favours me.
BYAM   I grudge him nothing this time, but if fortune
Had favoured me in the last sale, Clemene
Would be mine.

TREFRY	Are you still smitten by her?
BYAM	Every day more in love with her.
TREFRY	[*to* STANMORE]
	Captain, who is this Prince that's fallen
	To my lot for the Lord Governor? Let me know
	Something about him, that I may treat him
	Accordingly: who is he?
STANMORE	He's the Devil of a fellow, I can tell you,
	A *Prince* every inch of him. You have paid
	Dear enough for him, for all the good he'll
	Do you.
TREFRY	But who is he?
STANMORE	He is the grandson and heir to the throne
	Of the King of Coramantien, a mischievous
	Monarch in those parts, who would never
	Let any of his neighbours be quiet. This
	Son, Oroonoko, was his General, a fearsome
	Fighting fellow.
TREFRY	But if he's a Prince, why is he now a slave?
STANMORE	He was brought into my hands
	By the treachery of one of his father's own
	Ministers.
TREFRY	Is that his name, Oroonoko?
STANMORE	Yes, Oroonoko.
BYAM	[*as if trying it out on his tongue*] 'Oroonoko.'
STANMORE	I was forced to clap him in irons and
	Did not think the ship safe neither. He even
	Resolved that he and his followers
	Should perish for want of food. I had to give
	Him my solemn word as an Englishman that if
	Only he would relent from his resolve, and also
	Encourage his men to eat, I would allow him
	His freedom as soon as we reached Surinam.
TREFRY	But you have not done so – he is here
	In my lot.
STANMORE	Ah, sir, he was not to know it –
	But I kept my fingers crossed.

TREFRY   Captain, I'm afraid the world won't speak
          So honourably of this action of yours as
          You would have them.
STANMORE I have the money, let the world be damned.
          I have other matters to mind.

> [*Enter* OROONOKO *in chains, followed by other*
> SLAVES *including* ABOAN *and others of* OROONOKO's
> *warriors, all in chains and the very picture of*
> *dejection. They enter singing a lament, but sink into*
> *silence as soon as they see the white men.*]

OROONOKO [*to* STANMORE, *with sarcasm*] So, sir, you've set me free.
STANMORE [*bristles*] I am a better Christian, thank you,
          Than to keep my word with a heathen.
OROONOKO If your god teaches you to break
          Your word, I need not curse you.
          Let him cheat you.
          [*to* ABOAN] Whatever world we are next thrown
          Into cannot be worse than this. Farewell,
          My brother-warriors.
ABOAN AND SLAVES   Farewell, my General.

> [*Exit the* SLAVES, *including* ABOAN.]

STANMORE You see what a bloody pagan he is, Byam.
          I took care that none of his followers should
          Be in the same lot with him, for fear they
          Should undertake some desperate action,
          To the danger of the colony.
OROONOKO Live in fear; it is the villain's curse. Fear
          Even me who has no power to hurt you.
TREFRY   [*to* STANMORE] Take off his chains.

> [CAPTAIN STANMORE *makes a great show of being too*
> *busy lighting a pipe.*]

TREFRY   [*to* OROONOKO]
          The Lord Governor's on leave in England.
          You are his slave. In his absence it shall
          Be my duty to serve you. My name is Trefry.

[*He takes off* OROONOKO's *chains.*]

OROONOKO I am ready, where must I go? What slavish
Habit must I wear? Hard fare, and whips
And chains may overpower my flesh, and
Bow my body down but there's another
Part of me, out of your reach, which you
Can never kill.

STANMORE You have him, Trefry, and much may you
Do with your Prince.

[*Exit* CAPTAIN STANMORE.]

TREFRY You shall find nothing of this wretchedness
You apprehend. We are not monsters all.
I shall presume to call you Caesar.

OROONOKO I am myself, but you may call me what
You please.

BYAM A good name, Caesar.
And fit for his character.

OROONOKO Was Caesar then a slave?

BYAM He was a conqueror, but unfortunate in
His friends –

OROONOKO His friends were Christians?

TREFRY No.

OROONOKO No! That's strange.

BYAM [*leaving*] They murdered him.

OROONOKO I'd be Caesar then.
Do what you will with me.

BYAM We will, sir – depend on it.

[*Exit* BYAM.]

TREFRY When once our noble Lord Governor arrives
– He is a generous soul – I will tell him
Of Stanmore's double dealing. You may find that
He does all in his authority to find the
Means to send you home again to Coramantien.

OROONOKO I thank you, sir.
But my friends, sir, my honest, wretched
Friends! Their chains are heavy, they have

	Hardly found so kind a master.
	May I ask you, sir, what will become of them?
TREFRY	I'll use my best endeavours
	To see they're gently used.
OROONOKO	You tempt me to bid my hopes return, and
	Wait a better day.

[*looks despairingly at the moonless, bleak skies*]

Would you kill a dog because it barks, my God?
Would you kill a bull because it has horns?
Would you kill a parrot because its tail is red?

Let all those who are angered at me,
Let all those who are plotting against me,
Let them have no power over me,
Let them forgive me, no matter what I may have
Done amiss,
Let their anger subside, my God.

TREFRY I dare not ask you more than you're willing
To tell me. But if you think it convenient
To let me know your story,
I dare promise – if I can – to assist you.

OROONOKO Her name, sir, was Imoinda.
She died.
They killed her.

[*They exit.*]

Scene 2

A plantation: a few days later.

It is early evening, after a heavy storm.

Enter ABOAN *and other* SLAVES.

1ST SLAVE We must go back to work – if
The overseer catches us –
2ND SLAVE Shh – I hear him.
1ST SLAVE [*listens*] No, it's not him.
ABOAN Would he beat us then?

1ST SLAVE	*Would he?* Experience will Soon tell you that.
ABOAN	Has experience ever told you?
1ST SLAVE	I wish I could say no.
ABOAN	They've beaten you to silence – To patient drudgery.
1ST SLAVE	I'm ashamed to confess it.
ABOAN	You should be ashamed to Suffer it.
2ND SLAVE	We would not – if we knew How to help it.
ABOAN	Suppose a friend told you how?
1ST SLAVE	What do you say?
2ND SLAVE	How?
1ST SLAVE	Tell us.
ABOAN	I see you're not completely broken. I'll tell you news that'll string Your nerves anew.
SLAVES	[*all*] What news?
ABOAN	There's a mighty Prince, come among You now, a God in arms. Before his sword These pale, cold, half-formed tyrants would Vanish like mist before the sun.
1ST SLAVE	He came on your ship?
ABOAN	He came with me. I am myself Distinguished by his friendship. He will not bear this dull patience We suffer now.
2ND SLAVE	And will this Prince help us To be free?
ABOAN	If you will join hands with him –

[*Enter* OTMAN, *a slave from a neighbouring plantation, an angry-looking man.* ABOAN *does not know him.*]

[*As soon as he notices* OTMAN, ABOAN *launches into a chant and is quickly joined by those of his companions who know the chant and who also recognise it for what it actually is – a decoy to confuse this stranger –* OTMAN *– in their midst.*]

[ABOAN *and the other* SLAVES *gather in a circle,
around a log fire, holding one another's hands and
swaying gently in a ritual dance to Shango, the God
of thunder, and also the God of justice and fair play.*]

ABOAN   Be my guide, O Shango
          My God of thunder!
1ST SLAVE   You are the death
          That drips *to, to, to*
          Like indigo dye
          Dripping from a cloth.
2ND SLAVE   You are the leopard
          That kills the sheep –
3RD SLAVE   And bathes in its blood!
4TH SLAVE   You are a huge morsel:
          If anyone tried to swallow you –
ANOTHER SLAVE   – You'd be out of their anus
          Like lightning!
ANOTHER SLAVE   You do as you please, Shango
          My God of thunder!
ANOTHER SLAVE   Fire-eating masquerade,
          You frighten the big cat!
ANOTHER SLAVE   Invulnerable One:
          Who can behead a fly?
          Who can swallow a hedgehog?
ANOTHER SLAVE   You walk alone,
          But enter the town
          Like a swarm of locusts.
ANOTHER SLAVE   You are the King who knows
          Today – and tomorrow, too!
ANOTHER SLAVE   You've been known
          To make yam porridge
          From orange pips!
ANOTHER SLAVE   Even when you do not fight,
          Shango –
ANOTHER SLAVE   – We fear you!
ANOTHER SLAVE   But when war gleams
          In your eye –

SLAVES   [*all*] When war gleams
                In your eye, enemies
                And worshippers run alike!
ANOTHER SLAVE   Fire-in-the-Eye!
ANOTHER SLAVE   Fire-in-the-Mouth!
ANOTHER SLAVE   Fire-on-the-Roof!
SLAVES   [*all*] You ride fire like a horse!

> [*All through this* OTMAN *watches, with unconcealed
> disdain, and then leaves, shaking his head. He has
> hardly left when the* SLAVES *turn to one another.*]

ABOAN   Who was that?
1ST SLAVE   I've seen him about.
2ND SLAVE   I haven't.
1ST SLAVE   I have.
2ND SLAVE   I haven't.
ABOAN   Enough!
             Who is he?

> [*A* FEMALE SLAVE *steps forward.*]

FEMALE SLAVE   His name is Otman.
             He's owned by the Deputy Governor,
             Mr Byam.
ABOAN   What more do you know
             About him?
FEMALE SLAVE   He hates Mr Byam.
ABOAN   Why?
1ST SLAVE   [*as if it were self-evident*] Why else? Because Mr Byam
             Owns him.
ABOAN   Is he ill-used by Mr Byam?
FEMALE SLAVE   On occasion. But that is not
             Why Otman hates him.
ABOAN   Why does Otman hate him?
FEMALE SLAVE   Otman
             Hates him because Mr Byam is
             Known for a fool in the colony. When
             He's not drunk and raging like a
             Loon, he's to be found forcing himself on his

Female slaves and making brats
By the dozen. That's why Otman
Hates him

[*They hear a cry.*]

2ND SLAVE They whip a slave.
ABOAN [*thoughtfully*] Let's go back to work.

[*All exit.*]

Scene 3

The neighbouring plantation: later that night.

Enter PRINCESS IMOINDA *singing a sad, sad song.*

Enter BYAM *moments later, followed by* OTMAN *attending on him.*

OTMAN *is, all through the following, scrupulously servile and betrays nothing but deference to* BYAM.

BYAM I have disturbed you, I confess my fault,
My dear Clemene; but begin again.
And I will listen to your mournful song,
Sweet as the soft complaining nightingale's,
While every note calls out my soul and
Leaves me silent, as the midnight groves.
Sing, sing again and let me wonder at the
Many ways you have to ravish me.

IMOINDA I can weep enough for you, and me,
If that will please you.

BYAM You must not weep: I come to dry your tears,
And raise you from your sorrows.

IMOINDA How can that be, when everything you do
Convinces me that you'd keep me here,
Far from those I shed tears for?

BYAM Forget the past, Clemene. Look toward
Now, where better prospects rise,
And new pleasures court and invite you.

My heart has all the soft sensations
That love inspires –

IMOINDA Could your heart, forced to some distant land,
Unknown, forlorn, a slave, dependent on
Another's will, cut off from friends and family,
Could your heart forget all these?

BYAM Look at me, Clemene. I come to offer you
Your liberty, and be myself the slave. Do not
Turn away – [*follows her*] Let me hold this
Pretty hand, let me – I know your modesty
Would draw it back – but you would take it
Ill if I should let it go, I know you would. You
Shall be gently forced to please yourself; that
You will thank me for. But, if you struggle
With me, I must take –

IMOINDA You can take my life. I'll freely part with
That.

[*Exit* PRINCESS IMOINDA.]

[*Enter* CAPTAIN STANMORE.]

STANMORE So, Byam, I don't disturb you, I hope.
She's thankful for the honour of your attentions,
I suppose?

BYAM Quite insensible to all I say and do.
When I speak to her she sighs or
Weeps but never answers me as I
Would have her.

STANMORE There's something nearer than her
Slavery that touches her. What do
Her fellow slaves say of her?

BYAM Some of them, who hate her for being
Better used than they are, will needs
Have it that she is with child.

STANMORE Poor bitch. You cannot blame her if it
Be so.

BYAM I had Otman check on that.
Otman?

[OTMAN *bows.*]

OTMAN   Aye, master. I checked on that. She is not
        With child. She broods, they say, for her
        Husband.
BYAM   Her husband? What husband?

          [*They start as a sharp clang of alarm sounds in the
          distance.*]

          [*Enter* MR TREFRY *and* OROONOKO.]

TREFRY Make what haste you can, Deputy Governor,
        To save yourself and the colony.
BYAM   What's the matter?
TREFRY The Indians are come down on us.
        They have plundered some of the
        Plantations already, and are
        Marching this way as fast as they can.
BYAM   What can we do against them?
TREFRY We should be able to hold them back
        Until more planters arrive, if you would
        Show yourself and put us in order.
BYAM   Come with me, Trefry. You, Stanmore, stay
        Here and look after the slaves.

          [*As* MR TREFRY *and* BYAM *begin to leave, together
          with* OTMAN, CAPTAIN STANMORE *seizes* OROONOKO.]

TREFRY   [*turning back*] What are you doing?
STANMORE Securing the purchase.
          He is an enemy of the state.
OROONOKO My constant friend.
STANMORE He has the malice of a slave in him
          And would be glad to be cutting
          His masters' throats.
TREFRY   Let go of him.
          [*to* BYAM] He's in my care, I shall answer
          With my life for his behaviour.

          [*We hear the sound of Indian drums and soft flutes
          approaching.*]

TREFRY   Hell and the Devil! They drive away
             Our slaves before our eyes. Deputy Governor,
             Can you stand tamely by and suffer this?
             Your mistress, Clemene, is among them.

BYAM   [*in despair*] We're outnumbered and will throw
             Ourselves away, in the attempt to rescue
             Them.

OROONOKO   Give me a sword. I'll deserve your trust.

        [MR TREFRY *hesitates then hands him a sword.*]

OROONOKO   Follow me.

        [*All exit.*]

        [*Enter the* SLAVES, *fleeing for their lives.*]

        [*Enter the* INDIANS, *in pursuit of the* SLAVES.]

        [*Exit the* SLAVES.]

        [*Enter* OROONOKO, *in pursuit of the* INDIANS.]

        [*Blackout.*]

        [*Exit the* INDIANS, *pursued by* OROONOKO.]

        [*Lights up.*]

        [*Enter* BYAM, MR TREFRY, CAPTAIN STANMORE *and*
        OTMAN.]

        [*Enter* OROONOKO.]

        [BYAM *grabs* OROONOKO *in a grateful hug and a firm
        handshake.*]

BYAM   Accept our general thanks, Prince Oroonoko, you're
             Something greater save than Caesar ever was.
             What we can do more to recompense such
             Noble services you shall command.

        [*Enter* PRINCESS IMOINDA.]

BYAM   Clemene too shall thank you – she is safe.
             [*to* PRINCESS IMOINDA] Come, my dear, and bless
             Your brave deliverer.

[PRINCESS IMOINDA *and* OROONOKO *both look up and recognise each other at the same time.* PRINCESS IMOINDA *gasps.*]

OROONOKO   [*blinks*] Do not mock me, O Gods of my fathers,
Do not mock me with this illusion.

BYAM   What does he stare at?

OTMAN   It would seem, master,
He's her husband.

BYAM   Husband? How so?

IMOINDA   [*in a breathless whisper*] Is it really you, my Prince?

OROONOKO   Imoinda, you're – alive?

IMOINDA   I am – now, my husband.

[*They fly into each other's arms.*]

STANMORE   [*with great pleasure*]
Where's your mistress now, Byam?

BYAM   Why, where most men's mistresses
Are forced to be sometimes,
With her husband, it seems.

TREFRY   [*to* OROONOKO] Sir, I do most heartily congratulate
Your happiness.

BYAM   And all of us. But how did it all – ?

OROONOKO   That will require more time
Than I can spare you now. I have
A thousand things to ask her –

IMOINDA   And I, many more to know of you.

OROONOKO   This little spot of earth you stand
Upon means more to me than the green
Vastness of my father's Kingdom.
Your love is my Empire, and my heart,
Princess, is your throne.

[*All exit.*]

Act Two

Scene 1

The first plantation: later that same night.

The SLAVES are singing as they go home from a long day's work.

Enter OTMAN, bristling with rage.

OTMAN   What's wrong with you all? This is no time
        To look to the past. This is no time to dream
        Memories! It's time to think of *now*!

        [ABOAN *looks at* OTMAN.]

ABOAN   What do you know about *now*?

OTMAN   That we're slaves! Slaves to cowards!
        Slaves to rogues who can't even defend
        Themselves!

ABOAN   [*to* 1ST SLAVE, *whispers*]
        He talks as if he knows our purpose.

OTMAN   Go on, sneak in corners, whisper so your
        Masters don't hear you. Cringe and crouch
        Under the whip, like dogs licking their wounds.
        I feel as much as you feel, but I won't groan.
        As long as I have life and tongue I'll curse
        Them all.

ABOAN   [*to* OTMAN] Have you been long a slave?

OTMAN   Many years.

ABOAN   And what do you do, except curse?

OTMAN   What else can I do? I am but one man.
        If only someone with a soul of fire, a leader
        Of men, were to come forward and make a
        Body of us all, then I shall do something more
        Than curse.

ABOAN   You'd better be the legs of such a body,
        To make it march?

OTMAN   I'll be the heart of it – the head, the hand,
        And the heart of it!
ABOAN   [*to* SLAVES] I like this spirit, we need more like him.
        [*to* OTMAN] I may yet hold you up to that.

        [*Enter* MR TREFRY.]

        [OTMAN *stares stonily at him.*]

TREFRY [*to* ABOAN] Are you Aboan?
ABOAN   I have been called by that sound.
TREFRY Follow me.

        [*All exit.*]

                    Scene 2

The neighbouring plantation: that same night.

Enter OROONOKO *and* PRINCESS IMOINDA.

OROONOKO   Eshu, the trickster-God, came walking
           Once along a path between two farms.
           He wore a hat that was white on one side,
           Red on the other. The two farmers on either side
           Of his path saw him walk past. Later
           That day, as they drank palm wine together,
           One said to the other:
IMOINDA   [*as the farmer, laughs*] 'Did you see
           That odd man, in a white hat, who walked
           Past the farm today?'
OROONOKO   'I did see the man,' said
           The other, 'but his hat was red.
           I saw it with my
           Own two eyes.'
IMOINDA   'Well, then,' said the first farmer,
           'You must be blind.'
OROONOKO   'You,' responded the other,
           'Must be drunk.' The argument went on and the
           Two friends came to blows.

They became sworn enemies. The
King heard about the quarrel and sent for them.
Eshu was there at the trial and when the Kabiyesi
Could not apportion blame or praise, the trickster
Divinity revealed himself and showed the
Hat. 'Pardon them,' he told the King, 'they
Could not help but quarrel.
I wanted it so –'

OROONOKO AND IMOINDA [*together, laughing*]
'Spreading strife is my greatest joy.'

OROONOKO   When I heard you were dead, my Princess,
And then that scoundrel Stanmore kidnapped
Me, I thought the trickster-God had
Twice in one day mocked me with a cruel joke.
But I see now what my God was doing. Eshu knew you
Were not dead; he knew you'd been brought
Here and he knew that to bring us back together
He had to bring me here as well. Now, my Queen,
We can go back to Coramantien and resume the
    throne.
If we guess the future by the past
Our fortunes must be wonderful.

IMOINDA   [*unsure*] Good or bad, it must be in extremes.
Extremely happy or –

OROONOKO   It's in our power to make it happy now.

IMOINDA   But not to keep it that way.

[*Enter* MR TREFRY *and* ABOAN.]

TREFRY   I have a present for you.

OROONOKO AND IMOINDA   Aboan!

ABOAN   [*starts when he sees* PRINCESS IMOINDA]
Princess Imoinda!
We thought you were dead!

[*He falls at her feet in greeting.*]

OROONOKO   Orombo lied to us. He did sell her
To Stanmore.

	[*to* TREFRY] We all thought she was dead.
	How shall I thank you, my friend?
TREFRY	Trust me, and that would
	Be more than enough.
	I have seen to it that all your followers
	Will be gently used. This gentleman, your
	Chief favourite, sir, shall wait on you
	During your stay in Surinam.
OROONOKO	I owe everything to you.
TREFRY	You must not think you are in slavery.
OROONOKO	I do not find I am.
TREFRY	Your deliverance shall soon come.
	In the meantime,
	[*pulls* OROONOKO *aside*]
	You have enemies. People that represent you
	Dangerous and would be glad to find
	A reason, in your discontent, to fear.
	They watch your looks.
OROONOKO	I thank you for the caution.
TREFRY	I will leave you.
	Be assured, I wish you liberty.

[*Exit* MR TREFRY.]

ABOAN	He thinks highly of you.
OROONOKO	He means us well.
ABOAN	Are you sure, my Lord?
OROONOKO	Am I sure? What's to be gained
	From doubting?
ABOAN	You shield yourself from disappointment.

[PRINCESS IMOINDA *pulls* ONOONOKO *closer to her.*]

OROONOKO	We must be patient.
ABOAN	[*testily*] My King, as our fortune stands,
	There is a passion that would become
	You better than your love – Forgive me,
	My Princess, but I must say this ...
	A great resentment which, if inspired by you,
	Might kindle and diffuse a searing rage

	Among the slaves,
	To rouse and shake
	Our chains, and our struggle to be free.
OROONOKO	How can we help ourselves?
ABOAN	[*disappointed*] How can we help ourselves?
	I knew you when you would
	Have found a way. We need only stand
	Up to them, as the Indians have done.
	We have enough hands ready to be employed,
	Double the number of our masters' forces.
OROONOKO	[*dismissive*] What's holding you back?
ABOAN	[*ignores the sarcasm*] We need you – to lead us.
OROONOKO	You're in jest, Aboan.
	What would we do?
ABOAN	Cut their throats.
OROONOKO	And you would have me join
	In this murderous conspiracy?
ABOAN	It deserves a better name.
	It's called self-defence, my King.
	And natural liberty.
OROONOKO	I'll hear no more of it.
ABOAN	I'm sorry to hear that.
OROONOKO	Nor shall you think any more of it.
ABOAN	Not think of it!
OROONOKO	And that's an order, warrior.
ABOAN	Not think of it! Since the first moment they
	Put on my chains, I've thought of nothing
	But the weight of them. Goodnight, Princess.
	[*deliberately*] You, sir, are yourself a slave.

[*He begins to leave.*]

OROONOKO	[*shocked at the discourtesy*]
	You will not leave until I say so, warrior.
ABOAN	Try and stop me, slave.
IMOINDA	Aboan!

[ABOAN *turns back. He is weeping with rage.*]

OROONOKO   Remember this, Aboan, if we are
Slaves, these planters did not make us slaves.
They were not to know of Stanmore's treachery.
They bought us in an honest way of trade
As we have done before them, bought
And sold many a wretch and never
Thought it wrong. They paid our price
For us and we are now their property,
A part of their estate, to manage as they
Please. Mistake me not: I do not tamely
Say that we should bear all they could
Lay upon us, but we find the load so
Light, so little to be felt – considering they
Have us in their power and may inflict what
Grievances they please – we ought not to
Complain.

ABOAN   [*to* PRINCESS IMOINDA]
If you saw the bloody cruelties this people
Inflict on us – the poorest dog here is treated
Better than any of us –

OROONOKO   [*despondently*] I know that, Aboan.
And I wish I could honestly do more.

ABOAN   You must do more, and may with honesty.
Remember who you are, my General, a Prince,
Born for the good of other men, whose god-like
Office is to draw the sword against oppression
And set free mankind.
I know they claim to think highly of you,
And that they've promised you freedom.
But think what it is to wait on the promises
Of men who have always lied to us.

OROONOKO   Trefry is an honest man.

ABOAN   I do not doubt his honesty,
And I'm sure he means all he says.
But he's only one man in a government
Where you have many enemies.
What have they to gain by freeing you?

IMOINDA   He does make a point.

ABOAN   I know that you've been persuaded
          To believe that the Governor's arrival
          Will prevent any mischief and bring
          You liberty. But who is sure of that?
OROONOKO [*brusquely*] Summon your men.
ABOAN   [*jubilant*] You will lead us?
OROONOKO [*dryly*] You underestimate your powers
          Of persuasion, Aboan.
ABOAN   O Gods! Thank you, my Lord, thank you!
OROONOKO There'll be this reservation however.
          There will be no butchery. It would be wrong
          To break the ties of honour through fear others
          Should break them first.

          [*Exit* ABOAN.]

          [OROONOKO *turns to* PRINCESS IMOINDA.]

OROONOKO Is it wise?
IMOINDA   It isn't foolish.

          [OROONOKO *and* PRINCESS IMOINDA *exit.*]

          Scene 3

The first plantation: later that night.

Enter ABOAN *and* OTMAN *in mid-conversation.*

OTMAN   I don't like the sound of it.
ABOAN   I know how you feel. But is freedom,
          Without the loss of lives, not worth
          Accepting?
OTMAN   To our pale lords, perhaps, who only dare
          Strike those whom others bind, it might
          Be acceptable. But not to me. I thirst for more than
          Freedom. I want revenge. Let me think on it.

          [ABOAN *and* OTMAN *exit.*]

Scene 4

The neighbouring plantation: later still that night.

Enter OROONOKO, PRINCESS IMOINDA *and the other* SLAVES.

OROONOKO   Impossible! Nothing's impossible.
              We know our strength only by being tried.

1ST SLAVE   Great sir, we have heard you
              With great joy and admiration.
              But we have wives and children
              Who are unfit for such an expedition.
              What must become of them?

              [*Enter* ABOAN *and* OTMAN.]

OROONOKO   We cannot wrong the virtue of our
              Women to believe there is a wife among
              Them that would refuse to share her husband's
              Fortune. While we live and have our limbs,
              We can take care of them.
              I still propose we lead our march down
              To the sea and plant a colony where we shall
              Live free and able to defend ourselves till stress
              Of weather or some accident provide a ship
              For us.

IMOINDA   An accident!
              The luckiest accident presents itself.
              The very ship that brought us and
              Made us slaves swims in the river still.

SLAVES   [*all*] Let's seize it!

OROONOKO   It shall be so.
              There is a justice in it that pleases me.
              [*to* OTMAN] You do not relish it.

OTMAN   [*gingerly*] I am afraid you'll find it difficult
              And dangerous.

ABOAN   Dangerous! I thought you didn't know
              The word danger, you who would be the
              Head, the hand, and heart. Sir, I remember
              You, you can talk well. I do not doubt you
              Shall keep your word.

OROONOKO   [*aside, to* ABOAN] This man is not right.
             I'll try him further.
             [*to* OTMAN] The danger will be certain to all of us.
             We must expect no mercy if we fail,
             It's either liberty or death.
             There's no man here, I hope, who does
             Not come prepared for all that befall him.

ABOAN   If there be one among us who can fear
             The face of death appearing like a friend
             As this cause of honour death must be, how
             Will he tremble when he sees death dressed
             In the wild fury of our enemies in all the
             Terrors of their cruelty?

OTMAN   [*trembling*] What will become of us?

[OROONOKO *and* ABOAN *exchange looks.*]

OROONOKO   I could die altogether, like a man,
             As you, and you, and you, and all
             Of us may do: but who can promise
             Bravery when tortured on the rack,
             His skin flayed off and roasted yet
             Alive? The quivering flesh torn from
             His broken bones by burning pincers?
             Who can bear these pains?

OTMAN   They – they're not to be borne.

OROONOKO   You see him now, this man of mighty
             Words!

ABOAN   I cannot believe it.
             Such a blaze, and not a spark of fire!
             What shall we do with him?

OROONOKO   We are not safe with him.

ABOAN   Do you think so?

OROONOKO   He'll betray us.

ABOAN   That he shan't.

[ABOAN *goes to stab* OTMAN. OROONOKO *stops him.*]

OROONOKO   Are you mad? His murder would
             Alarm all the rest, and make them think

We're barbarians. We'll not set out
In blood.
We have, my friends, this night to furnish
What we can provide for our security and just
Defence. If there's any one among us we suspect
Of baseness or vile fear, it will become our
Common care to have our eyes on him.

> [*The* SLAVES *turn and stare at* OTMAN.]
>
> [*Exit* OTMAN, *fleeing.*]
>
> [*Exit* 1ST SLAVE *in pursuit of* OTMAN.]
>
> [*All exit.*]

Scene 5

DEPUTY GOVERNOR BYAM's *house: later that night.*

Enter BYAM *and* CAPTAIN STANMORE, *followed by a breathless* OTMAN.

BYAM   To seize the boat, you say?
OTMAN   Yes, my Lord.
STANMORE   At what hour?
OTMAN   Sometime tonight.
BYAM   Didn't they trust you?
OTMAN   They did, but then the Prince –
BYAM   Caesar?

> [OTMAN *nods.*]

Your honest service to the government
Shall be rewarded with your liberty.
I shall order all the militia under arms
Directly.

> [OTMAN *stands still and does not respond.*]

BYAM   [*puzzled*] What do you want, Otman?
OTMAN   [*after a quiet pause*] My liberty.
BYAM   How many hands have you
On deck tonight, Captain?

STANMORE	Enough to do the business.
	[*slowly turns round*] Deputy Governor?
BYAM	Yes, Captain?
STANMORE	I thought I caught the hint
	Of a glint in your eyes.
BYAM	[*irritably*] What? What?
STANMORE	[*smiles*] I thought I caught you thinking
	About your mistress.
BYAM	[*gruffly*] Nonsense, Captain.
	That's all in the past.
	She will hang together with her
	– [*mockingly*] Prince.

[*All exit.*]

Scene 6

The first plantation: later that night.

Enter OROONOKO, ABOAN, PRINCESS IMOINDA *and other* SLAVES.

OROONOKO	Come friends, the moon will rise soon.
	We must be swift and silent. We'll surprise
	The ship and win without loss of blood.

[*Enter* 1ST SLAVE, *breathless.*]

1ST SLAVE	Otman has betrayed us.
ABOAN	No!
1ST SLAVE	I saw him go into the Deputy Governor's house.
	The boat has now moved
	Farther from the shore. The
	Captain and his crew are up in
	Arms, all the planters are out and –

[*Enter* BYAM *with* OTMAN *and several other* MEN.]

ABOAN	[*bitterly, to* OROONOKO]
	Forgive me, my Lord, for trusting that slave.

[*He eyes* OTMAN *murderously and makes to attack him.*]

OROONOKO   Hold, Aboan.
          [*to* BYAM] Withdraw your men.
    BYAM   What can you do even if we did withdraw?
          Where will you go? What more can you
          Resolve? Be sensible, sir, you are outnumbered,
          Surrounded. Save yourself, throw down your arms.

          [*The* SLAVES *begin to panic.*]

    BYAM   [*to the* SLAVES] To everyone of you seduced
          Into this foolish act, we offer a full pardon.

          [OROONOKO *prepares to fight.*]

          [*The* SLAVES *desert him and rush to* BYAM.]

  SLAVES   [*all*] Pardon, mercy, pardon!

          [*Enter* MR TREFRY.]

    BYAM   I'm asking you to give up, sir,
          Before it is too late. Give up now
          And you shall have whatever terms
          You propose for you and yours.
          Talk to him, Trefry.
OROONOKO   Have you too come against me?

          [MR TREFRY *in reply pulls out his sword and lays it on
          the ground.*]

OROONOKO   I know what I have done.
          I'd be a fool to think I'd walk free.
    BYAM   [*to* TREFRY] Offer him what you will.
          I'll confirm and make it good.
  TREFRY   The Deputy Governor offers you unconditional
          Pardon, for you and yours.
          [*looks from* PRINCESS IMOINDA *to* OROONOKO]
          Sir, don't throw away the happiness
          You've just found, I beseech you.

          [OROONOKO *looks at* PRINCESS IMOINDA. *She nods,
          slowly.* OROONOKO *puts down his sword.*]

OROONOKO   We are in your hands.
    BYAM   [*to* STANMORE *and* OTMAN] Chain him.

TREFRY   You cannot mean –
BYAM   This is not your concern.
          Chain him.

> [OROONOKO *is seized.*]

> [ABOAN, *without warning, leaps at* OTMAN *and slashes him across the throat with a swift flick of his dagger.*]

> [OTMAN *dies.*]

> [BYAM *looks on, shocked.*]

> [ABOAN *is seized.*]

BYAM   [*to his* MEN] Dispose of them.
          [*to* PRINCESS IMOINDA] I must take care of you.

> [PRINCESS IMOINDA *stumbles and falls as if by accident. She quickly picks up the dagger with which* ABOAN *had killed* OTMAN *and hides it on her person.*]

> [*All exit.*]

Act Three

Scene 1

DEPUTY GOVERNOR BYAM's *house: later that night.*

Enter BYAM *and* MR TREFRY.

BYAM   The public good requires that he should die.
        The planters want him hanged.

TREFRY   Have you no reverence of future fame?
        If you confess humanity, and believe there is
        A God, to punish or reward our doings here,
        Do not provoke your fate. The Hand of Heaven
        Armed against these cries with hotter thunderbolts,
        Prepared to shoot, and nail you to the earth, a sad
        Example, a monument of faithless infamy.

BYAM   Tell me no more of fame and breach of faith!

TREFRY   He gave himself up. Remember, sir,
        He yielded on your word. Your word!
        Which honest men will think should
        Be the last resort of truth and trust on earth.
        Give him his liberty, sir, and I'll be his surety.
        I will answer for him.
        My friend, the Lord Governor, will thank you.

BYAM   [*relents*] You know where he's kept.
        Send a slave. Send word I ordered the release.

        [*Exit* MR TREFRY.]

        [BYAM *pauses a moment then opens a door leading
        into an inner room.* PRINCESS IMOINDA *is revealed,
        motionless, as if in a trance.*]

        [BYAM *seizes her.*]

BYAM   Come here.
        I'll no longer court you.
        The man that asks deserves to be denied.

[PRINCESS IMOINDA *pulls out the concealed dagger and stabs* BYAM *in the shoulder. He reels back in shock.*]

[*Enter* MR TREFRY.]

IMOINDA He does indeed, that asks unworthily.

TREFRY You heard her, sir: that asks unworthily.

BYAM You are no judge.

TREFRY I am of my own slave.

BYAM I granted your wish.
Why did you come back?

TREFRY To take the Princess with me
To see her husband.

BYAM Get out, leave us alone.

TREFRY When you let her go.

[BYAM *and* MR TREFRY *draw swords.*]

[PRINCESS IMOINDA *flees, the bloodied dagger still clenched in her fist.*]

[BYAM *swings his sword at* MR TREFRY. MR TREFRY *easily parries. He knocks the sword out of* BYAM's *hand, then bends to pick it up and return it to him.*]

[BYAM *pulls out a pistol and swings it down on* MR TREFRY's *head.* MR TREFRY *slumps down unconscious.*]

BYAM She shall not escape me. I've gone
Too far not to go farther.

[*Exit* BYAM.]

Scene 2

The first plantation: later that night.

Enter OROONOKO *chained to a post, followed by* ABOAN, *who is all bloodied up.*

OROONOKO Aboan! My ever faithful friend!
You're gashed and mangled.

ABOAN   [*lies down*] The hangman's hand would have
           Been kinder than what they did to me.

OROONOKO   I'm sorry, Aboan.

ABOAN   I do not come for pity, my Lord.

OROONOKO   Let me attend to your wounds.

ABOAN   [*laughs weakly*] That won't be necessary, my Lord.
           I dragged myself all this way to beg
           To be discharged.

OROONOKO   What can I do for you, Aboan?

ABOAN   My soul is tired and I have no strength
           Left in my body. I want, with your
           Permission, to leave this world.

OROONOKO   If I cannot provide you with an honourable
           Means of life, the least I can do is to bestow
           You with an honest means of death. Here.

           [OROONOKO *gives* ABOAN *a dagger.*]

ABOAN   I cannot stay to thank you.
           I shall not say farewell.
           [*stabs himself*] I shall wait for you
           In the next world, my Lord.

           [*He dies.*]

OROONOKO   Farewell, my friend.

           [*Enter* PRINCESS IMOINDA, *running.*]

OROONOKO   Who chases you, my Princess?

IMOINDA   It's in vain to call him villain.

OROONOKO   Call him Byam. It is Byam, isn't it?

IMOINDA   There isn't another man so vile.

OROONOKO   What has he done to you?

IMOINDA   I cringe to think about it.

OROONOKO   What did he do?

IMOINDA   What he could, he dared.

OROONOKO   May his own gods damn him.

IMOINDA   That worthy man, your friend –

OROONOKO   Trefry.

IMOINDA   Trefry came in and saved me
From the Deputy Governor's rage.
[*She is very frightened.*]
You must promise never to see me
Forced from you again.
[*sees* ABOAN] Aboan!

> [OROONOKO *reaches for the dagger in* PRINCESS
> IMOINDA'*s hand and makes to stab himself in the
> stomach.*]

IMOINDA   [*stays his hand*] You cannot leave me here all alone.
We must go on this journey together.

> [*They hold in a tight embrace.*]

IMOINDA   Be quick, make haste,
Our enemies have eyes.

> [*They kiss*]

IMOINDA   I'm ready.
OROONOKO   [*listlessly*] I can't.

> [*She takes up the dagger.*]

IMOINDA   Then I must assist you –

> [*As she makes to stab herself,* OROONOKO *stays her
> hand, takes the dagger away, and grabs her in a tight
> embrace. They hold onto each other as if for dear life.
> Then, in one swift movement,* OROONOKO *breaks her
> neck.*]

> [*She dies immediately.*]

> [OROONOKO *holds onto her, and weeps bitterly,
> violently. He reaches for the dagger and makes to stab
> himself in the stomach.*]

> [*Enter* BYAM *together with* CAPTAIN STANMORE.
> *both armed with shotguns.* BYAM *is still bleeding. He
> looks ashen, ill, at death's door.*]

[BYAM *sees* PRINCESS IMOINDA's *body. He goes and examines her, sees she's dead.*]

BYAM   [*gasps*] Who did this, Caesar?

OROONOKO   I, Byam, I killed her.

[*Enter* MR TREFRY *armed with a shotgun.*]

BYAM   [*raises his gun*] He shall die.

TREFRY   [*raises his gun and points it at* BYAM] He shan't. Leave.

BYAM   Do you threaten me, Trefry?

TREFRY   Tell him to leave, Stanmore.

STANMORE   Come, Byam, let's leave.

[*Exit* BYAM, *practically carried by* CAPTAIN STANMORE.]

TREFRY   [*to* OROONOKO] I'd come with news.
The Lord Governor has arrived,
This past hour, from England.
He has agreed to give you liberty.

OROONOKO   [*looks at* PRINCESS IMOINDA] It's too late.

TREFRY   No, it's not.

[OROONOKO *raises the dagger, to stab himself.*]

TREFRY   Don't, Oroonoko.

[MR TREFRY *begins to raise his gun.*]

TREFRY   I shall not let this happen.

OROONOKO   Leave, Trefry.

TREFRY   No, sir.

[MR TREFRY *takes aim at* OROONOKO.]

OROONOKO   Very well, then, you leave me no choice.

[OROONOKO *charges towards* MR TREFRY *with every intention of stabbing him.*]

[MR TREFRY *hesitates, then he shoots* OROONOKO.]

[OROONOKO *falls down.*]

[MR TREFRY *runs over to him.*]

TREFRY   Oroonoko!

[OROONOKO *dies.*]

[MR TREFRY *remains standing in the same spot, looking suddenly very tired.*]

[*The sun begins to rise.*]

[*A slaves' lament rises with the sun.*]

[*Black.*]

THE END

Other plays by 'Biyi Bandele

MARCHING FOR FAUSA

Presented at the Royal Court Theatre and winner of the award for Best New Play at the 1994 London New Play Festival.

" 'Biyi Bandele's first full-length play simply crackles with anger and dark laughter. It is a story of terror and corruption in an African state: a journalist investigates a shady cabinet minister with predictable results. It's as if Dario Fo had written a fiery and ferocious political parable. Highly recommended." *John Peter, The Sunday Times*

"A powerful play about the evils of dictatorship."
Michael Billington, The Guardian

DEATH CATCHES THE HUNTER
and ME AND THE BOYS

Death catches the hunter with pain.
The trickster-God catches the herbalist in a sack

Presented by Wild Iris at the Battersea Arts Centre in 1995, *Death Catches the Hunter* is the lyrically comic tale of a prophet, a teacher and a garage mechanic, wide-boys and spiritual power, adoration and the desire for revenge.

" 'Biyi Bandele has written a parable for three voices about faith, manipulation, self-deception and credulity. . .There is both a political and a spiritual lesson in this agile and original play, and Bandele's writing bristles with snide, irreverent and intelligent humour."
John Peter, The Sunday Times

"A wry meditation on the art of storytelling."
Kate Stratton, Time Out

* * *

For 'Biyi Bandele the Nigerian oral tradition is like jazz. "You take a familiar motif," he says, "and then you improvise around it. You re-imagine it." In *Me and the Boys* two young men share a prison cell. "Sit back, relax, let me tell you a story," says Kas. "There were five of us. . ."

Other plays by 'Biyi Bandele

RESURRECTIONS

In *Resurrections*, presented by Talawa Theatre Company at the Cochrane Theatre in 1994, ancestral spirits blur the edges of reality for businessman, barrister and beggar. Motive, memory and morality are all strangely ambiguous in this, the season of the longest drought.

"Bandele is an extraordinarily talented writer who needs no special pleading. *Resurrections* is a work which resonates with ideas about history and heroism, set in a modern-day African state where ancient legends still abide. Drug dealers, lawyers, ghosts and vultures mingle on stage, and all seem equally convincing... 'This is Kafka on speed,' says one of the confused spirits. Actually, it's much better than Kafka. *Resurrections* is a visual and verbal treat from a gifted writer still at the beginning of what will doubtless be a long and fruitful career."
Louise Doughty, The Mail on Sunday

TWO HORSEMEN

Presented at the Gate Theatre in 1994.

"In *Two Horsemen* 'Biyi Bandele writes sympathetically about imaginative escape from drudgery. Two men in a hut while away the time talking. They say they are street-sweepers, but gradually they slither away from reality, swapping identities and repeating passages of dialogue until you have no idea who they are, what is the truth and whether they are alive or dead. Bandele's writing is exciting, enigmatic and disturbing – like Beckett and Pinter, he manages to use dramatic dialogue to create an unsettling slippery world."
Sarah Hemming, The Independent

"The joy of this play is in the slow realisation of its mythical depths ... Reminiscent of Beckett and Soyinka, this is a thrilling piece of writing."
Clare Bayley, Time Out

For a free copy of our complete list of plays and theatre books write to:
Amber Lane Press, Church Street, Charlbury, Oxon OX7 3PR
Telephone and fax: 01608 810024